Empath and Psychic Abilities

Stop Empathic Burnout, Awaken Your Third Eye, Supercharge Your Psychic Skills, and Engage Your Innate Power to Thrive

S.C. Rowse

© Copyright 2022 - All rights reserved.

The content contained within this book may not be reproduced, duplicated or transmitted without direct written permission from the author or the publisher.

Under no circumstances will any blame or legal responsibility be held against the publisher, or author, for any damages, reparation, or monetary loss due to the information contained within this book, either directly or indirectly.

Legal Notice:

This book is copyright protected. It is only for personal use. You cannot amend, distribute, sell, use, quote or paraphrase any part, or the content within this book, without the consent of the author or publisher.

Disclaimer Notice:

Please note the information contained within this document is for educational and entertainment purposes only. All effort has been executed to present accurate, up to date, reliable, complete information. No warranties of any kind are declared or implied. Readers acknowledge that the author is not engaged in the rendering of legal, financial, medical or professional advice. The content within this book has been derived from various sources. Please consult a licensed professional before attempting any techniques outlined in this book.

By reading this document, the reader agrees that under no circumstances is the author responsible for any losses, direct or indirect, that are incurred as a result of the use of the information contained within this document, including, but not limited to, errors, omissions, or inaccuracies.

Table of Contents

Introduction 10

   Before the Start 12

Part I: A Closer Look at Empaths 14

   Chapter 1: Empaths in the Spotlight 16

      Explaining Empathy 19

      What It Means to Be an Empath 25

      Random Facts About Empaths 31

      Leading the Way to Meditate 34

      What's Next? 36

   Chapter 2: The Anatomy of an Empath 38

      Traits of an Empath 39

      When It Comes to Others 42

      What You Get With an Empath 45

      The Bright Side of Being an Empath 45

      And the Dark Times 47

      Affirmation Meditation 49

      What's Next? 50

Part II: The Empowered Empath 52

Chapter 3: Unleashing the Power Within 54

Powerful Empathic Abilities..56

Activating Your Empathic Powers 58

White Light Meditation 63

What's Next? 65

Chapter 4: Intuition 66

Intuitive Empath: A Review 69

Tuning In..77

What's Next? 79

Chapter 5: Aura Reading 84

What Is an Aura? 86

What Happens in an Aura Reading?..........................90

Reading Auras... 91

Healing Auras 93

The Steps of Restoring...94

What's Next? 95

Chapter 6: Telepathy 96

What Is It, Anyway?...98

A Telepathic Empath 99

Namaste Telepathy 103

What's Next? 104

Chapter 7: Clairvoyance 106

Clairvoyance 109

Seeing Better 111

Visualization Meditation 112

What's Next? 114

Part III: An Empath's Guide to Self-Care 116

Chapter 8: Unblocking and Balancing Chakras 118

Chakras 120

When Chakras Get Clogged 126

Chakra Contemplation 131

What's Next? 132

Chapter 9: Cleansing and Healing Your Energy 134

Why Clean Inside 136

Tools and Toiletries 137

Cleansing Meditation 146

What's Next? 147

Chapter 10: Protecting Yourself as an Empath 148

Things That Drain an Empath 150

Signs That an Empath Is Burned Out 151

How to Protect Yourself 152

Protection Meditation 153

What's Next? 154

Conclusion **156**

References 160

Image References 178

Empaths did not come into this world to be victims; we came to be warriors. Be brave. Stay strong. —Anthon St. Maarten

Introduction

Today, I wish to reminisce on the life of a little girl who had it hard growing up. Not an easy life, to say the least. Her mother, you see, had given herself away to booze.

"Your mother wasn't always like this," she remembers her father saying. At that time, she wanted nothing more than to believe him, but all she knew was her mother and the bottle. They became inseparable views. Her father was never home, always traveling for work and handling business elsewhere; anywhere but home. His addiction was money.

So, while her mother drank and her father sealed deals, she was left alone to care for her younger siblings. She was the eldest, after all. Therefore, the duty and responsibility fell on her alone. She did what she had to do.

Her mother dragged herself to the same bar night after night, sleeping away the days, drinking glass after glass of whatever she could... Until it drowned her. Can you imagine that? Walking the same line every night, drinking yourself into a haze, until one day, the bottle runs out, and you just never wake up again... They buried her mother and soon her father remarried.

His new wife was a narcissist who believed that "no one is as good, or as worthy, as my children and I!" She was an awful woman, and for a moment or two, the little girl couldn't help but wonder what her father had seen in such a self-absorbed ogre. You might think that's harsh, but if you knew her, you might say it's too kind.

It was during this time that her life took a turn for the worse, and since her father had only ears and cares for his new wife, his children were, once again, left alone to tug out their own aches and hardships.

Instead, the little girl enveloped herself in coping mechanisms and found comfort in books. The local library became her sanctuary. It was a place where she lost herself between the pages that told stories of the world, human psychology, and of empaths and their unique abilities. Why these topics? you ask.

Well, it seemed that something good had come from the years of heartache, longing, and despair after all. As a teenager, she soon realized that she was different from the rest of her peers. Call it a hunch or the subtle discrepancies she felt tugging on her coat. Turns out, she was right.

Somewhere along the road, as she pushed and pulled to cope and make it on her own, the world around her started to vibrate beneath her feet, allowing her to feel every inch of it move and breathe. From the wrangles came a gift: her empathic abilities.

From there, a dedication grew, sparked by her curiosity and desire for the empathic globe and nature. She spent every waking minute learning as much as she could. It became much more than a simple coping tool; it became her purpose in life. She realized that her trauma, although part of her, did not define her and that it had significance. Every single unpleasant bump or slashing helped push her toward a life of her own, a life that she was proud of.

Today, she's helping other people find their place and peace within this world, a reason for them to feel contentment within themselves. A hypnotherapist and author. A proud and dedicated woman hoping to share all she had learned from those trips to the library. She hopes to guide those around her where she can. Just as she wished someone had done for her when she was just a child, alone and unsure in this world and within her individuality...

Today, I wished to reminisce about a little girl. Today, I wanted to tell you about myself.

Before the Start

Empaths make up only a slim percentage of the world, which means that, as an empath, you have few resources and advice to guide you through what you're experiencing, why you're feeling particular ways, and doing certain things differently. It can be a scary and confusing time, and this is especially when you need all the help and support you can get. Luckily, we're in a different age, where within a single click you can reach anyone or anything, including the information you need to finally understand who you are and how to be who you're meant to be.

Living in a world that is full of pulsing energy, negativity, and close-minded folk can be hard. People believe in certain things and have set-in-stone opinions and views. It can be hard to find your way between all the chaos and uncertainties. You might be familiar with questions like these: Why do I feel so much of everything all the time? It's my fault for being so sensitive, isn't it? Why don't my relationships stick? Did I push them away? Did I look into their lives too deeply? Why am I not like them? What's wrong with me?

The answer, my dear reader, is simple: you have done nothing wrong. You're simply unique. Being an empath is a gift, and the sooner you realize that, the better. However, I know that's easier said than done! Luckily for you, I was once in the same boat, and I've dedicated my life to this very moment: to help you through it all.

I know right now you don't see an outcome that looks so good or peppy, but you will soon. With this read, I strive to help you overcome your feelings of being overwhelmed and unsure while you take back your power and reclaim your life as your own. You'll finally be able to answer these questions, understand what it means to be an empath, and feel empowered in all you are.

You will be equipped with the information and tools you need to develop and enhance your powers as an empath: your intuition, ability to read auras, telepathy, clairvoyance, chakra healing, and energy cleansing. You'll also read about how to protect yourself and live life freely.

I can sit here promising you a better life where you have a greater understanding of yourself and your powers, with confidence big enough to take on the world. However, the outcome is in your hands. You're already taking the proper steps toward trekking into your light and genuine self. So, what do you say, empath? Are you ready to take this journey and see what you got?

Part I:
A Closer Look at Empaths

Chapter 1:
Empaths in the Spotlight

She was born in a small town, one of those where your neighbor is the art teacher, camp counselor, and clergy all rolled into one. Everyone knows everyone, shares the same views, and no one ever strayed far from their parents' and grandparents' usual routes and ways. I guess you can say, "It runs in the family" was the town's motto, and it's one the people followed proudly at all times.

She was a born and raised Christian, with set-in-stone religious beliefs and sturdy faith in church. However, that's precisely where her dilemma stemmed...

As a Christian, she felt, sensed, and experienced things that some members in her church would have called evil. What if she were to be frowned upon in her religion? Were her "gifts" but a curse? A taboo of some sort that was unacceptable to have and hold? It felt like she was walking a different route and paving her own ways, which in her opinion, was steering her in the wrong direction.

Walking this desolate route left her feeling alone more often than not, as if she was taking steps no one else had ever taken, and there was no one to turn to for miles. She was ultimately alone and alienated, even when she was the one to blame for her isolation. In her mind, these things happening to her were wrong, after all, so they had to be pushed away.

For decades, she tried ignoring her thoughts, feelings, and experiences as they came into her life, but she never truly could stop herself from wondering about them. Although it took her some time to accept, she finally gained the guts, confidence, and strength to open up about her senses and become the person she was meant to be.

However, she had many obstacles to go through before she found herself: She faced challenges and strange ordeals that she didn't know how to deal with. But she did.

Her earliest experience was with a janitor at her elementary school, Jake. She didn't know how to explain it. It was almost like they were two magnets and the magnetic field connecting them was his feelings. However, whatever emotion Jake was wearing on his sleeves that day, she felt twice as hard.

One day before the school term ended, she spotted Jake sitting against a wall during recess. She somehow knew he was feeling glum, so she strode over to him and asked what bothered him. Jake simply shook it off, stating that he was sad to see them leave and that he would miss them while they were away for the summer. It was clear that he didn't want to be alone and that having the children and staff around made him feel at home and comforted.

She (barely) held back tears the rest of the day, even when they painted butterflies in class, and all through her car ride home, and even until she went to bed. And maybe even a little more when she woke the next morning. She was only eight at the time, but what she was experiencing seemed so… adult.

So, here she was, experiencing others' feelings. It wasn't one of those relatable moments like "I get where you're coming from"—she was genuinely handling and partaking in their emotions as if they were her own. She knew she was experiencing something others weren't. She was terrified, yet very curious at the same time. These experiences continued, and so did her time with Jake.

She wanted to explore this feeling further and get to the bottom of what was happening to her. It became an extracurricular class, a course that lasted most of her life. During her research and study, it was once again Jake who steered her toward another ability she had: She could guide Jake toward things he lost.

One day during recess, she saw Jake looking for something, his eyes darting around on the ground. He had lost his earphones and had run the school ragged looking for them. When they talked, she directed him to a classroom on the second floor. She didn't know how she knew, but somehow she was sure they were there. On the other hand, he was confident that they weren't as he had not been there that day. To his surprise, they had been there all along! He found them set neatly on one of the front row desks. Jake simply forgot that he had cleaned up a mess earlier that morning and must have set them down as he moved the bucket and mop.

Isn't that neat? Imagine not having to search around for your keys or phone ever again! However, she never again sensed things quite that clearly. Those two experiences were just the tip of the empathic iceberg, and all she could do was sit along for the ride.

As her life went on, she found that her dreams allowed her to communicate with people and that she could talk to others nonverbally. At the same time, she could predict parts of her future, observe and hear people's thoughts, intervene with occurrences, sense events, and share the burdens of others. She had this sense of knowing some things without being aware of how they came to be; she called it the "knowing." When these abilities popped into her life, she felt happy sometimes, and scared and uncertain in others.

However, throughout the years, she knew that her abilities didn't have to hold her back, even through the uncertainties and chaotic, overwhelming times. Still, she found a way to help others; that's all she could ever have wanted. The novel path she had strayed onto when she was just a child was different than she initially expected or wanted. However, it was her path and she was glad she had taken the time to walk it.

Her name is Emily, and she's an empath.

Explaining Empathy

Have you ever heard the expression of putting yourself in someone else's shoes? It's a common saying, but a flawless definition of what empathy is. It's about lacing up another person's footwear and understanding their emotional state, thoughts, intentions, and experiences as if you were the one experiencing them first hand.

Let's say you slip on a pair of boots covered in mud and shredded foliage, with a few rips and tears. Perhaps there's even a chunk of bubblegum on the heel. When empathetic toward that person, you need to step into and take on it all: the dirt, grass, wear and tear, and even that muddled piece of pink gum. You have to be compassionate and understanding no matter what they carry on their soles or how much the boot might smell. It's about genuinely connecting with someone, taking the time to understand them, and building a meaningful relationship, whether emotional, cognitive, personal, or professional. You're not only stepping into their shoes, but into the person they are.

You adjoin your life with theirs, no matter how good or bad your own circumstances are, and live a day (or even a second) as someone else. You feel, understand, see, and open up to others. Only then will you truly feel and comprehend empathy.

The Science Behind the Word

As humans, we're often in search of answers and reasons behind things, a science that can give us an explanation for specific occurrences and abilities. Call it human nature, modern society, or whatever—it's just how we're programmed to think, act, and respond. When it comes to understanding empathy and empaths, our character and reasoning are no different: We want to know what these words mean and how they work. Ultimately, we want to know the science behind them.

Here's the problem: Once you tackle the research, you stumble upon countless pieces of information that are all conspiracies and possibilities. This is simply because there's a lack of research and science to back up how these things work. Hence, while we run through the information, you should remember that some of it might be debunked, further elaborated, or irrelevant in the future. Still, it won't hurt to do a bit of diving of our own, will it?

Research, even if not fully complete, can help us gain a new perspective and understanding of what makes up these words. Even if, at the end of the day, they only act as a foundation for us to build on as we move along, it will still be an interesting read and perspective on things at least. As Karla McLaren stated in her book, *The Art of Empathy* (2013):

> "Empathy is everywhere: it's the air you breathe and the ground you walk on; it makes relationships, communities, and societies work. And yet, empathy can also be something of a mystery. Because empathy is such a central part of everything you do, you can overlook it and almost ignore the processes that make empathy work (or stop working). This is actually an important part of how empathy functions, because you don't want to have to think about every piece of empathic information you pick up, then catalog all of it, then reflect on each piece, and then plod through all of your possible responses. In fact, it's good that empathy is generally hidden from your conscious notice! But when you want to consciously work with your empathy—either to increase it or to calm it down—it's very important to be able to enter into that hidden world and understand the processes of empathy very clearly." (pp. 7–8)

Clearly understanding what empathy is and how it ties in with us is paramount for developing and improving our empathic abilities.

We need to know these things to build meaningful relationships of our own, understand ourselves and others, and finally be at peace with feeling empathy.

Science Explains

So, we know there isn't much backbone to the science behind empathy and empaths, as a great deal of the information revolves around the basics, speculation, tell tales, and assumptions. Therefore, I thought we couldn't rely on a single explanation alone, so after some further research, I have three...

Neurons Holding Mirrors

Brain cells make us work the right way. Some parts of the brain are responsible for memory, others for sleep, emotions, etc. You could say that everything we do is due to certain features or cells in our brains firing away and doing their chores. Researchers believe that the group of brain cells responsible for compassion also enables us to mirror emotions and share the feelings of others.

Think about when you watch a cooking show, and your gut starts panging with hunger and cravings during the program, all because you were influenced by the delicious treats and meals.

Hence, is it really such a stretch to say that emotions, experiences, and people can also direct and influence our mannerisms, actions, and emotions? I would say that it's not impossible and could even be likely. Well, this is precisely what the theory suggests.

Think of it this way: Like the image below, we're all walking through life with a large mirror pointing outward toward others. Whenever we catch something's reflection, we mirror that image, whether it be an emotion, feeling, or experience. Like when you grab a snack after watching a chef cook on TV, you think, act, and respond after seeing someone upset, happy, or in pain. With this theory, researchers believe we show empathy and compassion because we trigger our mirror neurons and reflect that person within ourselves.

Imagine seeing a loved one upset and how much it hurts you to see them that way; those dark clouds are roaring their reflection into your mirror. The same goes for when you see your child happy and playing in their own little world; you would be ecstatic, wouldn't you? Reflections, mirroring, and echoing—that's what it's all about.

Theoretically, it makes sense, but it might not translate into real life situations. If someone bawls in front of you, no matter who they are, you likely won't burst out laughing or break out in dance. Then again, that could also be seen simply as common decency.

The theory does explain some aspects of empathy and why we feel it, but it doesn't cover all the grounds. Emily, for example, shared what Jake, the janitor, felt at all times, even when they weren't near one another. You can't mirror something that has no reflection. Thus, some gaps within the theory still need to be filled.

The Power Line

Can you recall how I compared Emily and Jake to magnets? Well, that statement was much more than a comparison; it's actually a theory behind our empathy, but the magnet has a shocking twist to it... literally.

Researchers believe that electromagnetic fields are generated in our brains and hearts, which shoot out information about our thoughts and feelings to others. It's almost like we're all a part of a major power line that constantly surges and sparks out pieces of ourselves.

We send out various information depending on our different feelings and experiences at all times. When we're optimistic, for example, we'll send out a different message than the one when we're pessimistic. The range of waves and emotions go on.

However, there's not much research on this theory and it leaves many unanswered questions, like how far the frequency can get or whether there are set patterns and facts behind the theory.

Shots of Dopamine

The next theory has to do with another part of our brains; this time, it has to do with a neurotransmitter and hormone called dopamine. Dopamine is a messenger between our neurons and is often called our "happy hormone" since it's responsible for our happiness, among other things. It's that feeling you get when you're doing something you find enjoyable, participating in a fun event, or you're over the moon about something happening. In short, it's that extra kick of pleasure you get every now and then.

Now, what does dopamine have to do with empathy? Research shows that different dopamine levels can influence our sensitivity to it. You feel things more deeply than others would when you have high levels of dopamine, and not only when it comes to yourself. Therefore, when you hop on a water slide, you catch more dopamine from others. When their dopamine levels drop, you experience that drop with them.

What to Think

It seems like all three theories have a common theme: They focus on explaining how we feel empathy up close. However, they never answer how we feel sympathy over distances, or how empaths like Emily can sense and understand the burdens of others without as much as a sniffle. Still, even when the science isn't up-to-date, we're lucky to have so many spiritual people to help us move forward.

What It Means to Be an Empath

Empaths are individuals who have a keen eye toward the needs and well-being of others. They feel others' feelings, emotions, and physical symptoms, unable to separate them from their own. People like Emily see the world from a different perspective and often find it hard to simply step past others.

Empaths often find it hard to pull themselves away from others as they're highly conscious of the presence and experiences of those around them. As an empath, you might struggle to internalize your own thoughts, feelings, and experiences, due to this disturbance. You can say others get in the way, but you don't mind because you've already laced up a new pair of shoes to wear.

When viewed spiritually, being an empath can be seen as an intuitive, psychic ability that paves the way for connecting with others on a deeper, more meaningful level. You understand, take on, and recognize the mental or emotional state of others above all else, even at times when it doesn't seem appropriate.

It's about sticking to your gut, connecting and understanding others openly, and allowing yourself to feel and live beyond empathy.

Types of Empaths

We now know that being an empath means reflecting on the highs and lows of others. You, quite literally, wear your heart on your sleeves since there's nowhere else for it to go! That space in your chest is overpacked and often reserved for those around you. They're incredible individuals with an intense gift of tenderness and connection that they share with others. However, when it's misunderstood, unchecked, or overindulged, you often feel the ability drain you of yourself, your own feelings, and your life experiences. As a preventative measure against these self-burns, knowing what kind of empath you are could help you find your way through life. Yes, you heard me, there's a whole variety of empaths, and you could even be more than one.

Psychic Empath

Empaths who are described as "psychic" or "medium" are those who have a keen and unique understanding and appreciation for the afterlife. Psychic empaths are people who have dropped the veil and allowed themselves to see into the spirit world and touch ground with people who are no longer with us. They can communicate, hear, see, and pick up on extrasensory energy from the afterlife. Afterward, they use these pieces of information to form conclusions and guide themselves and others in the real world.

Emotional Empath

We know that all empaths show a degree of heightened empathy toward the feelings and emotions of others. However, when it comes to emotional empaths, their ability to sense and read the emotional and mental state of others is their strongest, or singular, empathic trait.

Emotional empaths live in a world governed by the emotions of others, which could be difficult with all the negativity hanging around us these days. However, when surrounded by happy people and "good vibes," they might find themselves merely enjoying the ride.

Telepathic Empath

Telepathic empaths are like the rest, but they do it a little differently by reading other people's thoughts while also sensing their emotions. These empaths often use their senses and observation knacks to read their surroundings and the thoughts, feelings, and beliefs of those around them. You could say that they're the editors of others: They read the manuscripts of those around them and help them tweak, brush up, and rewrite the chapters of their lives, or even just a mere paragraph of the day.

Physical Empath

Do you know how seeing someone smile or yawn automatically causes you to smile or yawn too? Well, imagine that feeling amplified by 50 (if not more)—that's precisely how physical empaths feel most of the time.

These are empaths with an enhanced sense of perceptiveness to the well-being and condition of others' bodies. They can, for example, sense a migraine coming from a mile away! Not only do they sense health concerns in others, but they often experience them too. They can also mimic a person's habits, tics, and mannerisms, such as twitching their eyes or tapping their fingers. It's about getting physical, or at least feeling the burn...

Psychometric Empath

Psychometric empaths gather information and energies from the objects and the places around them. They can connect the dots to the meanings and connections of the people associated with them. They get all their information right from the things around them and others.

Molecular Empath

When you think of something being at a molecular level, it means studying something up close, looking at every cell and fiber it holds. Molecular empaths are very similar in that they can see up close into a person's true nature. They can see into that person sleeping underneath all the years of layers, masks, and boosted egos humans often create.

Fauna Empath

Do you know someone who always hangs out with animals? Perhaps that's you. If it is, chances are you're a fauna or animal empath. No, I know your first instinct might be to assume that these empaths are the *Disney* princesses and *Doctor Dolittle's* of the world, but that's not quite right (although they understand animals so clearly that they might as well be).

Fauna empaths deeply understand animals' postures, expressions, and movements, allowing them to share a special connection with their furry friends. Sometimes, the lives of pets are closer to ours than we think.

Flora Empath

Just as animal empaths prefer hoofs and whiskers, flora empaths prefer spending their time with all things that blossom, bloom, grow, and sprout. These are all the green thumbs out there who don't only prefer crossing out their time with foliage, but can actually communicate and pick up on the energy and signals vegetation breathes out. They can keep plants living, growing, and thriving while warning them when in danger. They put the "guard" in gardener!

Geomantic Empath

If you didn't know any better, you would think that flora and geomantic, or earth, empaths are one and the same. Although similar, earth empaths are unique in their own ways. While flora empaths run around with the vines, geomantic empaths run through all the soils, winds, and earth. They're sensitive to the changes in the world, such as feeling shifts in energy before natural disasters, weather changes, and whenever the environment is harmed. They're one with the world, and the earth is one with them.

Indigo Empath

For starters, indigo empaths have nothing to do with the color or with feeling blue. Indigo empaths are very similar to molecular empaths. They can spot and know when someone's morals and virtues aren't as good as they claim to be. Morality and virtues are what they're all about. They usually stick to people who are truly good and have honest, moral purposes simply because they know who is who.

Claircognizant Empath

Claircognizant is quite the bite to say, isn't it? However, it's not tough to understand. If it makes things easier, you could call them intuitive empaths, which points straight to their instincts. These are people who could walk into a room and instantly know where everything is, or those like Emily who just know where things are without any evidence or reasoning behind their claims. They sense validities through leaps of logic and can pick up thoughts, feelings, and information (seemingly from nowhere) without any solid explanation. They also know what they should and shouldn't do and people's true intentions simply by evaluating the energy hovering around them.

Precognitive Empath

Precognitive or predictive empaths can feel a situation or event before it happens. They can see these predictions in dreams or extreme emotional or physical upheaval that some describe as being trance-like or like they're convulsing, which is often accompanied by bursts of anxiety and nervousness as their sensitivity intensifies.

Yes, to some degree, they can see the future of themselves, others, and the world in general, even when they don't always realize it. Call it what you will: psychic ability, intuition, or sensitivity to patterns. Still, somehow they just know what will happen…

Dream Empath

Have you ever woken up after a dream and could recall every single detail? It all felt so real and vivid. These are how dream empaths experience their sleep at all times. They recognize and interpret their dreams expertly while understanding the information and details their brains are trying to tell them. They remember and decipher the whole story from the start, the plot, and the finish, while also being able to decode and grasp the dreams of others. Counting sheep, for them, isn't all about pressing snooze. It's about immersing themselves in a new world where reading between the lines is fully encouraged.

Heyoka Empath

The "heyoka" is considered a spiritual fool in the Lokota and Dakota Native American culture. At first, I wouldn't have made the connection, but it makes sense when you understand what it means to be a heyoka empath. These empaths often heal and connect with others using humor, just like how a clown or fool uses humor to reinforce the statement that laughter is, in fact, the best medicine. These empaths are often unconventional in their thoughts, actions, and behaviors, such as poking fun at situations that change the perspective of others. They often force people to study and rethink their viewpoints, notions, experiences, and where they're currently standing in their own lives. Although sometimes they might not say what you want to hear, their remarks and observations might just do you a favor.

The Most Important Thing

So, we have now discussed all the forms of empaths. However, I wanted to take the time to highlight the fact that you can, most definitely, be more than one empath.

Take Emily, for example: From the summary of her life experiences, we know she definitely has more than one empathic ability in her corner. She displays signs of being an emotional, claircognizant, dream, precognitive, and telepathic empath most of her days—and you could too.

You know yourself best, and you've lived your experiences firsthand; therefore, you will see whether you're an empath of one sort or have a whole bucket to carry around. Trust yourself and evaluate your life and situations where and when you can to see what you might discover about your empathetic self.

Random Facts About Empaths

Random facts have the power to turn everything around and make everyone go, *ooh*! There's just something about them, I'm telling you. Thus, I couldn't resist throwing in some of our own regarding empathy and the people who feel it.

Little Helpers

If you were to sit behind a one-way mirror to observe the world, you would note that behind closed doors, people tend to be a little more selfish. However, when empathy comes into play, selfishness starts to fade.

Research by the University of Oxford revealed that people with higher levels of empathy were quicker to learn when helping others. Researchers gathered up a variety of people and suggested a game: Participants got two different symbols; one carried higher chances of winning points, and the other not so much. They were asked to play for themselves and on behalf of another person. Players then had to choose between the two different symbols; choosing the "big earners" correctly (through trial and error) would churn points into money. These were the results:

Brain activities from the participants higher in empathy lit up in a region believed to drive our learning when seeking the best results for others. It showed that some people are at their best when they have others working as their motivation. Since empaths embody empathy, they might just have that additional *oomph* of drive to give others a helping hand where they can. It's in their nature, after all.

Painkillers Kill

Pain killers were meant to kill any pain we might feel; I mean, it says it all in the name. However, a study has shown that paracetamol, a common ingredient in pain meds, might dull out much more than a simple headache. That's right! Researchers found that pain relievers temporarily block out your empathy. Let's say you're having a spat with a friend, and no matter what you do, you can't see or understand what you did wrong. Well, you might have to blame the paracetamol! Doses of the painkiller could make it harder for you to catch onto the feelings and emotions of others, even when you would usually understand or sympathize with them.

Within the study, groups had to read short stories where people got stabbed to the bone, and someone's father died. People on pain meds thought it wasn't that big of a deal. The impact is quite scary, right? Although uncertain about why the medication had these effects, they theorized that it had to do with our brains. A comparable study conducted in 2004 supported that the part within our brains which activates when we experience pain also starts up when others are hurting. Therefore, when we put two and two together: We see that dulling out our own discomforts causes our other sensations, like compassion, to dim as well.

So, empaths, I know sometimes popping a painkiller seems like the right thing to do, but why not try and stick to the more natural remedies from now on?

The Gaps We Have

A study of discrimination in our every day, researched at the University of Milano-Bicocca, found that people react differently to pain, especially when it comes from someone who isn't the "same."

Groups were, for example, shown clips of needles hitting skin, and their reactions were closely surveyed. Whenever the group's skin color was pierced, they reacted far more dramatically than when a needle touched the skin of someone of different ethnicity. No, it doesn't mean that the entire group was racist. Some people might assume, for example, that one race, due to previous misfortunes, are hardened and less sensitive to pain. This concept is often called the "racial empathy gap." Perhaps, these groups connected the clips to their own skin, thereby feeling as if it were their own hand they were seeing and not the skin of someone else. However, it doesn't matter as it's anything but true. Researchers reasoned that their reactions were merely due to their thoughts, beliefs, and attitudes toward privilege and hardships.

Another gap we have regards gender. Men are often criticized for wearing their hearts on their sleeves or showing empathy and care toward others. However, men are perfectly capable of being empathic, even more so than some women.

Although the blame in these gaps falls onto the opinions and influences of the world and our shared histories, they are, and remain, absurd! Gender, ethnicity, location, and anything else you can think of, are irrelevant. Empathy knows no such thing, and it doesn't discriminate. It's about heart, compassion, and genuinely tending to and considering the needs and feelings of anyone and everyone, as it should be. Empathy should just be about empathy.

Leading the Way to Meditate

Empathic abilities are gifts. However, sometimes the hits you can take often make them feel like a curse. When you sponge up all the negative and toxic emotions and energies of others or when all the varieties of emotions clog up, things become overwhelming and tiring. We're left in a rut that we often struggle to climb out of, which benefits no one.

Thus, as an empath, you must find ways to protect yourself from the emotions of others and the strain they put on you. It will allow you to take control of your empathy to better show compassion toward yourself and others in the future. Ensure that you do things the right way without burning yourself out.

Guided Meditation

Step One:

Move into a safe, supportive, and comfortable environment where you're away from others and can't hear, see, or sense them. Be mindful of your surroundings and find a spot that will allow you to truly be alone.

Ensure that you have a welcoming, warm, and compassionate presence and attitude so that you can connect with your most authentic self. You could light up some candles, ease into some cushions, or dim the lights if you feel that it would contribute to a relaxing atmosphere.

Step Two:

Ground yourself by straightening your spine and slightly lowering your chin. Now, take deep breaths through the nose and gently push them out your mouth. Focus on your breathing and follow each breath as it moves throughout your body.

Relax into yourself, mind and body, taking as much time as you need. If you lose focus at any time during the general relaxation, recenter your thoughts and pull the focus back to breathing. Remember, there's no need to feel guilty about focusing on yourself. You deserve adoration and compassion. Remind yourself that, "I deserve love" and that "peace surrounds me," and just breathe.

Step Three:

Think about the burdens, thoughts, and emotions you hold, those of yourself and others. Visualize the people, moments, and circumstances you absorbed. Remember what you're holding onto.

Now, slowly allow them to leak out and drip from your mind and body, and see the people wave you goodbye and all the events being laid to rest. Make your visualizations as vivid and realistic as possible, and finally, let go of the baggage you're carrying.

See how these empty crevices fill with peace, harmony, and positivity—from the top of your head to the tips of your toes.

If you're drifting from the image, breathe and bring your attention back to the visions. Remind yourself, "I can do this," and "It's okay for me to release all my negative energy and the energy of others."

Focus on your breathing and your affirmation as you visualize the scene and fully experience it as best you can. Don't worry about guilt and distractions; just be present with your imagery and nothing else.

Keep it there as long as you want and return to the present whenever you're ready. Take your time and work at your own pace. Whenever you're done, slowly roll out your shoulders, stretch your limbs, and take a last breath.

If you encounter an unpleasant or traumatizing memory during meditation, it's important not to run away from the negative energy.

I know this can be hard, but be with it and stay in it; it will dissolve on its own. It also helps to journal afterward.

What's Next?

Even though we've covered plenty of ground throughout this chapter, there's still plenty of information to dig through. Besides, we haven't even scratched the surface of your trait, so keep calm and read on!

Chapter 2:
The Anatomy of an Empath

"A curious child," people would tell you if you asked them about David. He's always been that way, though. When he was just six years old, you would not find him without a good book in hand (albeit a relatively simple read with a lot of pictures). He found atlases especially favorable. They interested him, as learning often did; he would trace his finger along the borders, asking his parents what the figures meant. "Continents," they would explain. He hadn't learned it in school yet, and the idea of different people, cultures, and routines interested him deeply. He would further ask them what foods those people ate and what languages they spoke, putting forward as many questions as he could. One day, he swore he would travel to them, eat all those foods, learn their tongues, and get to know the people who lived within those shapes. He wanted to travel and feed his observant curiosity of what the world held.

David had a strong sense of self, always knowing what he wanted. He noticed, relatively early in his life, that he could feel every inch of the planet. The world, it seemed, was his greatest and oldest friend, and he was drawn to every bit of it: the energy, the food, and the different environments. It was as if the planet was, somehow, breathing under him, whispering tales about itself and the inhabitants it held.

Growing up, he knew he wanted nothing more than to help others. He found it uplifting and rewarding, giving those drawn to him in their time of need solutions and helping them become the most empowered versions of themselves.

He felt comfortable sitting with the pain, suffering, and dark periods of others' lives. He always made time to understand their emotions, relationships with others, with food, with fitness, and their own character. He became good at this—holding open spaces for those around him. He became fueled by his gift and observations and moved to Los Angeles to start his own business, where he became a personal trainer and nutritional coach in hopes of bringing a new perspective to his clients and adding value to their lives.

However, he made sure to always remember the little boy he once was: the observant, questioning, self-sure, and curious six-year-old. Whenever he needed a break from all his life demands, he would take time to himself; he would sit on the yellow, sharp grass outside, feet folded, with an atlas laid out under his nose. He would trace the borders of the continents gently, listening as the world whispered some of its tales again.

Traits of an Empath

When the world around you moves differently and you view things and display emotions and feelings at different rhythms, it makes sense why you would question what an empath is and whether you're one yourself. Luckily, research hasn't let us down on that one, and there are some signs and traits of what it means to be an empath that could help you dot the i's and cross the t's of what it means.

Personal Space

Empaths are, for the most part, quite introverted. Of course, not all of them are, but more often than not, they prefer spending time alone as being overly social might make their battery leak.

If you think about it, empaths trying to keep to themselves isn't a far-fetched statement. They absorb and feel the emotions and energies of others while also trying to balance their own thoughts and feelings.

Think about a balloon filled with water, with empaths being the balloons and water being all they absorb. Now, imagine adding more and more water (emotions, thoughts, and the behaviors of people, animals, and even plants) to the balloon. Inevitably, the rubber will stop stretching, and eventually, the balloon just *pops*! This is precisely how most empaths feel when overwhelmed.

Empaths are sensitive and "absorbent" to the emotions, motivations, feelings, and circumstances of others. But not just that, they also take in and feel every inch of what's around them: certain sounds, fragrances, lights, and just about everything and anything else you could think of. All the energy around them, whether from people or places, gets snatched up and added to their balloons.

Furthermore, because empaths are so easily distracted by every person in distress, their surroundings (especially when harmful), the masses, "fake" people (which they can sniff out), and others, they tend to burst under the pressure of all they've absorbed. Empaths are sensitive to the world around them because it takes a significant hit on their battery packs, leaving them drained in the aftermath of simply being who they are. It's a lot.

Therefore, many empaths tend to isolate themselves after spending time around many people, in unsuited environments, or around "energy vampires." They must take time to themselves, engrossed in nature, surrounded by animals, or simply by catching up on some of their hobbies. They need to recoup, gather up their own thoughts and emotions, work through those of others, and get back into the right state of mind.

It's an essential part of learning to cope, to work through what you absorb, and to live with the occasional "burnout," which happens only to the best of us.

That Gut Feel

Einstein once described intuition as the only "valuable thing." Well, empaths have plenty of intuition to go around! If your intuition is on the higher side, you'll know that when your gut comes talking, you listen closely. Empaths are often known for their highly tuned "gut feeling," which is almost a regular for some.

Those with their gut already set in stone understand what a gift intuition truly is. Empaths grow comfortable with their own feelings and those of others; they know who they are, so much so that when "that feeling" comes along, they trust it because it knows best.

Intuition lies within those moments where you just know things (and you don't quite know how); when you're a walking detective or lie detector sniffing out the true intentions and motives of others; when red flags rise and white ones wave. No matter when you get them, you learn to trust that "itch" because it's gotten you this far, and when you lead with your gut, everything else just seems to fall right into place.

At the same time, some empaths might need tweaking, rehearsing, and willingness before they can genuinely unlock, understand and listen to their intuition. Some empaths might hit higher on their intuitive score simply because we, as a species, want to fit in with the crowd. Life's already pretty confusing, sometimes even more so for a child who views the world differently and acts "strange." It can be challenging for an empathic child to blend in with the crowds. And when they display abilities, it's a sure way of not getting a seat at the lunch table (or that's what children often think, at least). Instead, they bury their abilities in hopes of protecting their own energies, as well as their reputations.

When they grow up, however, they learn to accept the kinks of their personality and awaken those gifts that slipped away. So, you're not a "weaker" empath, you've only jumped off the starting line later in life. It's nothing a bit of practice, meditation, and gut-feel can't fix!

When It Comes to Others

Running off what we've covered this far, we know that empaths feel what others feel, and they're quicker and more accurate when it comes to noticing the emotions of others. They care deeply, genuinely, and with all their hearts. It's just who they are. However, empaths do a lot more than just feel and hug.

The Pull

Empaths live for others and would do anything to please others and keep them from getting upset, even when it means they often get the worst cards in the deck. But, don't get me wrong, they aren't puppies that go around doing what others tell them, sniffing out someone to please—not at all.

Empaths are simply wired to think and react differently than others, which isn't a bad thing. They're often the best people to have around, with the biggest hearts and most compassionate, honest, and supportive outlooks. They simply know which responses go where; they react with more tenderness toward those in distress, and those "inappropriate" statements and actions are much lower when an empath has the last say in matters.

Empaths are like universal wall sockets that absorb all the negative energy and provide the plug or battery with all the voltage it needs. They know that by understanding and connecting with those around them, they can supply a healing environment in which they can leave fully charged. They're natural healers, listeners, and friends because that's how they were born.

Empaths aren't the only ones attracted to people in distress: When someone is experiencing problems, emotional turmoil, or other damaging punches, they flock to empaths like chickens to poultry feed.

To the outside world, empaths are seen as benevolent and patient listeners who understand the thoughts, emotions, sensations, and perspectives of those around them. They know what others are trying to say even when their words don't make sense or they haven't made a peep. They can just throw the best advice your way because they can easily slip into your shoes and situation. It's no marketing scheme; empaths are just that approachable!

If the problem happens to be a fight, you can bet they'll do whatever they can to resolve conflicts. Empaths are known to be "lovers" and definitely not "fighters." They avoid conflicts and keep peace wherever they go, since arguments and disagreements cause distress and could even make them physically ill. Sometimes they can't even stomach cruel, aggressive, or upsetting things on the TV or in print!

Fights of any sort could be too hard for them to handle because they're so susceptible to the emotions and situations of others. Keeping things "real" and helping others get back on track in their relationships is an often must-do for them. So, if you get in a fight with an empath, or you're one yourself, try talking things out before you start shouting. Trust me, it's better for everyone involved.

Empaths are like a good tea to those around them and offer the ability to calm and heal while leaving them all warm and cozy. They have a presence like no other that could help others work past their severe emotional baggage and unhealthy patterns. They're the med-kits many need in their lives, and they wear their crosses right on their sleeves for others to see. So, therefore, it's no surprise why there's this pull between empaths and those in need.

Experiences Over Estates

Empaths know how to seal the deal on making others happy, especially since their choices are often hand-picked with others in mind. This is why empaths are more likely to try new things while giving others a skip, as long as everyone is happy. It's not that they're susceptible to peer pressure or anything; they simply value memories over materialistic things, and who wants a bad memory?

Social Struggles

We know that empaths are most comfortable one-on-one with someone, in smaller crowds, or all alone. However, comfortability doesn't always mean actuality. Their social preferences frequently collide and clash with other personality traits, such as the need to heal, listen, and the ability to feel and absorb what others are feeling. Nevertheless, empaths care for the well-being of others no matter what it takes, simply because their kindness comes naturally in abundance. I know it might sound strange, but this is precisely where the problem stems: Empaths are too generous.

Empaths often struggle with drawing a line, learning to say "no," and setting boundaries for themselves and others to follow. They hate to disappoint, especially since they're so involved in everything they do. When they say no, or put some space between themselves and someone else, they often feel guilty and as if they've failed with their gifts. It's not a fun thing to learn and do, but it's vital.

Without setting boundaries, they run a high risk of having the wrong people bite onto their line: those who wish to exploit and misuse their good nature. Not to mention the potential emotional and mental "burnout" or overload.

When they fall off the horse, they'll always point the finger inward, even when it's not their fault. Many empaths understand that their gifts come with consequences, such as strain on their stability and well-being after juggling everything from everyone else. In addition to this understanding, empaths are confident in who they are and at ease in their own skin. These near-opposites combine to create balance. This self-assurance allows them to easily stray away from the "blame game" and find stability and peace from within.

Still, the risks can't be ignored. Empaths have to know their limits, build boundaries, draw out their personal space, and learn to say that one simple word—*no*.

What You Get With an Empath

Empaths are exceptional folk with remarkable, often quirky, characteristics which make them one of a kind. One that stands out is their openness and honesty about who they are and how they think or feel. You could say they take "a penny for your thoughts" seriously or simply enjoy sharing part of themselves with others: an eye for an eye, or something like that. Either way, there's no guessing what you'll get with an empath because they tend to be themselves from the very first moment you meet them.

The Bright Side of Being an Empath

Telling an empath why being one is fantastic is like telling a child why presents are pretty cool: You don't have to because it simply goes without saying! However, this is a book, and what author would I be, and what guidance would I be offering, if I didn't lay it out for all the readers to see?

You know those colored building blocks almost everyone has stepped on? Well, empaths are the construction workers that can take a single block and turn it into a whole house or city, whichever one they prefer! They're individuals with the unique opportunity and capability to shift their lives and surroundings to their liking, all while offering those around them a safe haven and place of belonging.

Although the imagery might sound a bit extreme, when you see where I'm trying to go, you'll know just how fitting it really is. So, to give you more specifics, I have some bullets for you to read through:

- Empaths are like a fresh coat of paint on a wall that you, for some reason, paint every day. They just make things work and look good; they ensure that things are as balanced as they are pleasant. As mentioned throughout, empaths keep the peace among circles and groups; they listen well, care deeply, and make it their mission to ensure everyone's happy with themselves, their relationships, and overall lives. They live for others.
- Empaths are potent healers that others go to when needed, while also great at ensuring sturdy bonds. They build houses and communities from the brick up that are meaningful, peaceful, and long lasting. I don't know about you, but to me, that sounds like a splendid recipe for good vibes, spatial harmony, great get-togethers, and superb family dinners!
- Apart from being able to support and care for those around them, there are some additional benefits to being highly attuned to others. Empaths' natural intuitive abilities help them attract meaningful relationships from the start. This

hopefully means they'll stay away from toxic people and relationships that do them no good. Usually, they can spot when someone is good for them and when their intentions aren't coming from the best place. However, sometimes people and intents change, and you might find that someone who once meant good has turned their back on you and that some relations just weren't meant to be. However, that's not your fault; that's just humans.

- As I've said, empaths have a different, unique view of life that very few can grasp. They always have a fresh outlook, what more is there to say? They take on and live each day in their own little world with original (sometimes unusual) ideas, magnified emotions, with gifts and abilities that can pivot the lives of many, even the whole planet, if that's what they want. They live life with love and compassion like no other, have fun, feel sadness on a deeper level, see an ocean where there are deserts, and dance where there are no floors.

No matter how crazy my examples sound, empaths can do it all!

And the Dark Times

What goes up must come down; you can't get the good without going through the bad; every silver lining comes up behind a darker cloud, and all that stuff. All those sayings are true, and Uncle Ben from *Spiderman* might've had a good point when he said that "with great power comes great responsibility." When it comes to empaths, they have these big and wonderful abilities and gifts that can do so much, but as with most things in this world, it comes at a cost. Here are some of the downsides:

- While taking on all the positive, happier, and lighter emotions of others can be a blessing, empaths also have to take on and deal with all the not-so-good textures, sensations, and feelings. Unfortunately, they're often stuck in this tornado of negativity that leaves them sad, exhausted, anxious, and often defective in sharing their gifts with those in need. This is a problem as it's a rash most of them struggle to get rid of and keep under control. When empaths are dealt those heavy hands, they often find it hard to get back on track after being so easily distracted, overwhelmed, and burnt out. They would much rather take on the flowers and rainbows than the storms and clouds, but who wouldn't? Yet still, they do it without as much as a flinch.

- Just like the sales floor of every Wall Street movie, or almost all the call centers within the states, empaths are constantly surrounded by thousands of beeps and rings, running from phone line to phone line. Information is all around us: The earth exhibits its weather patterns, natural ways, and all the quirky, majestic, and mighty things that make it as it is; people are always thinking, on the move, and dealing with their own inquiries and paths; even inanimate objects have a thing or two to say (and that's just to mention a few). Empaths have open lines and toll-free hotlines to the world around them, meaning that most of the information running around goes straight to them. Gifts and capabilities aside, this could cause crossed lines and twisted wires: Empaths get confused regarding their own information, feelings, thoughts, and overall way of life. They're bombarded with the motivations and aspirations of others; their lives get intertwined, which can leave them blind to what there's to see, including their own life purpose, health, and personal roots and motivations.
- When people don't understand something, they often retaliate with conflict, punches, or some other form of defense. You could call it survival instincts in times of uncertainties. Therefore, as an empath, it's important to note and understand that your gifts and abilities will not be appreciated by everyone. Personal space and privacy has long been an essential part of individualism. Thus, when spaces get invaded and privacy gets broken, some people

won't be favorable, accepting, or take things in the right light. I know empaths rarely mean to be invasive and step on others' toes, but still, people won't always understand that, so be cautious about what you pick up and keep to yourself where needed.

Affirmation Meditation

Throughout this chapter, I have touched on empaths absorbing emotions and how it can cause you to be left with flat tires, drained batteries, and confusion on which parts and emotions go where. It's perfectly understandable how such a deep connection to the world around you can be overwhelming. Therefore, you need to set some tools and methods in place for when those moments creep up and you need some time to unwind and collect your thoughts.

The Script

Step One:

You know the drill already, so take your time to organize and set up a relaxing space that works for you and fits your comfortability. Then, take a seat on a pillow, mat, or wherever you like, straighten your spine, lower your chin, and relax into yourself.

Step Two:

Now, simply start breathing, just as before: in through the nose, out through the mouth, remaining calm and conscious as you do so. Focus on how your stomach and lungs rise with air and how your abdomen pushes out the warm gusts of wind. Imagine with each breath how your body sinks with ease as you take in positivity and spew out all your problems and those of others. Just breathe and relax.

Focus on nothing else. You can do it for a minute, or two, or more. Just keep breathing, however long you want. If you find yourself wondering, simply recenter, refocus, and get back to breathing. Remind yourself that you're in charge of your body, mind, and actions.

Step Three:

As you're breathing, slowly roll your focus onto your toes. Notice how they feel: Are they tense, sore, tight? Imagine them tightening and loosening up as you strip away their tension and pain, toe by toe.

Then, shift your emphasis upward, scanning your limbs bit by bit, all the way up to your temple. Focus on every fragment, how each part feels, and how you remove the stresses and problems they hold. Remember to breathe.

Step Four:

When you've completed the scan through your body, allow yourself a moment to sit and think. Note whether you're more aware of your body and how it feels, which emotions and pains belonged to you, and which were those of others. Remind yourself that it's okay and necessary for you to loosen up and let go of these strains and feelings, even when they belong to others. Know that you're in control. Continue breathing for a couple of seconds or until you're ready to return to the present in your own space.

What's Next?

We have now confirmed that being an empath is a gift worth looking after and that your traits are one of a kind, through good and bad. In the following chapters, we'll discuss and learn how you can harness your unique abilities as an empath to benefit yourself and others while living your life as best you can.

Part II:
The Empowered Empath

Chapter 3:
Unleashing the Power Within

Gusts of wind whirled through the air as Autumn plucked the leaves from trees and blew them onto the Montgomery driveway. In the kitchen window stood a woman peeking behind the curtain as an old beat-up truck made its way to her. It was Dylan, the Montgomery boy, on his way to see his parents.

It was particularly nippy that morning—weather Dylan had been waiting for since the start of fall. Pumpkin-spiced coffee... That was all he was after, and his mother made the best in Louisiana!!

He knew the drink was something very few were fond of, but to him, the beverage was why the season was his favorite.

Ecstatic to see her son, who was off at work most of the year, his mom had the drinks ready a good hour before his arrival and a pie that had been resting since early.

"Nothing the microwave can't fix!" she argued when Dylan's father had reasoned that it was better to wait until he got there. His words fell upon deaf ears as everything was ready, propped before the microwave, awaiting their spin.

Tires screeched to a stop outside, followed by heavy footsteps and the sound of the front door opening and shutting in the foyer.

"Mom! Dad!" a hurried voice called, peeking around every corner of the home, like an eager little child.

As he stumbled to the kitchen, his mother embraced him in a bear-like hug before discussions of work and life flew between the two. Shortly after, she retreated into the kitchen to warm the coffee and slices of pie while Dylan joined his father in the living room.

His father groaned as he sat upward. "I hurt my back at work. I'm getting too old for this darn work, I'm telling you!" He moaned, trying to sit comfortably without his back pain acting up.

Suddenly, Dylan got this overwhelming sense that he was able to help his father. He couldn't explain it, but he knew he could heal him, which was especially strange considering his field was nowhere near medicine or massage. Still, it was a hunch he couldn't ignore.

"I can fix that for you," Dylan stated, causing his dad to give him a skeptical glare. Even if he did believe him, he was in so much pain and didn't want to be touched. Yet, he gave way to Dylan's request to help, desperate for some sort of relief.

Dylan gestured for his father to slide onto his stomach and helped him pull the shirt over his head. He then grabbed the anti-inflammatory gel already standing on the coffee table, spewing a great deal of the cold goo onto his palms before working it onto his father's skin. He massaged the muscles for a few minutes, allowing his hands to guide him (since he had no idea what he was actually doing) until he thought his job was done, and told his father to stand.

He did so carefully, slowly moving around, expecting the pain to be the same as before. Much to his surprise, there was none, not even a single ache or cramp. He was healed.

With a maniacal laugh, his father jumped up, twisting, turning, and bending in all directions. He then ran to his wife, who had since stumbled from the kitchen, taking the tray from her hands and giving her a peck on the cheek. Laughing, she sat next to Dylan as his father took over handing out the coffee and plates.

Pumpkin-spiced coffee, Dylan thought, taking the warm mug between his palms, and with a slight sip, slowly relaxed into his chair. *I needed that now more than ever!*

Powerful Empathic Abilities

When empaths move through the world, they move differently, with a spring in their step, but that could just be the abilities talking. Empaths are graced with capacities and gifts that your average Joe doesn't have, whether good, bad, beneficial, or not. These allow them to help themselves, others, and the rest of the world. They're the proficient few, yet still, they're only trying to find their way in a world that's sometimes a hard nut to crack.

Seeing Clearly

Empaths can take on and see the world and scenarios around them from all perspectives. They aren't stopped by walls, brigades, and lies, because they can see right to the core of problems, conflicts, and situations. Call them four-eyes (without the glasses) or walking microscopes, but they can simply see clearer than most. Moreover, they're more likely to step up to the plate to find solutions to these crises. Their vision never ceases to amaze and never disappoints.

Intuitive Self

Since we've touched on intuition quite a bit, and there's still loads of information to come, I will keep things short. Intuition is a way of safeguarding the empath's energy and well-being. They walk with their gut, and everyone better listen when they feel something is wrong because they often know best, and their intuition never lets them down.

Long-Distance Empathy

Empaths care deeply, so much so that their compassion knows no distance. Even when someone is hundreds of miles away from them, they simply know when to give someone a call or when troubles are brewing on the other side of the world. They're most likely able to defy distance rules because of their firm and in-depth connection with others and the spaces around them. It's an unexplainable gift, but it sure beats wondering what's going on in someone's life and expensive trips to visit them.

Powerful Presence

There's a great power that empaths can make use of once they open themselves up to their gifts, abilities, and true nature. They can adjust their approaches to fit specific people's needs and deficiencies, healing them with a simple touch of their presence. However, it means that empaths really have to lay themself out there without any boundaries or limits, which explains why this is a rarely used trait reserved for loved ones.

Canny Career Choices

When you consider empaths' overall personalities, traits, abilities, and inclinations, we know that they're deep, sensitive, and nurturing souls with a knack for creativity and problem-solving. Therefore, it would make sense that they're drawn to careers in the arts, business, education, medicine, and other industries that help them express themselves and aid others. Empaths must choose their careers wisely while not sticking to traditional or unwanted paths if that's not what they truly want. It will suppress their true purpose in life and leave them never feeling quite right.

Spreading Zen

As we know, empaths are emotionally gifted and physically attuned to surrounding people and environments. They pick up batches of information that make it easier to make informed decisions, calculated responses, and precise plans of action to navigate and understand people, relationships, and situations. They're emotionally intelligent, and when they use it to their advantage, they can shift the vibes and circumstances of a room to make it work for their energies and lives.

Early Suppression

For those who know nothing about volcanoes, it might look like a mountain that bursts every now and again. However, behind the curtains, the earth's core is heating up and melting rocks left and right; this is called magma. Magma is pushed through vents and crevices up to the surface as volume and pressure build until it's too much, and the whole thing goes up in smoke. Emotions, anxiety, and personal struggles are very much the same. They start off simple, as rocks melting, but when overlooked, pressure starts to build, and before you know it, it's too late, and lava is all over the place. Empaths have the chance to pick up on these emotions and struggles (without being told) while still in their early stages. They can, for example, pick up on unusual tension among their friends, emotional distress in a colleague, or any other problems around them, and step in before things explode into something surreal.

Activating Your Empathic Powers

Some empaths are "born for greatness," but I stress the word *some*. Most empaths aren't born with rock-hard intuition, a killer ability to understand everything they're experiencing, or can ground themselves within a single flick of a thought. Unfortunately, real life isn't the movies, and we can't all have it figured out before we hit the half-mark.

More typically (and realistically), most empaths need to put in the work and time to train and nourish their skills and strength before they can turn them into superpowers. It's a bummer, I know, but it's also necessary, and you simply have to trust the process.

While growing up, most empaths develop and strengthen these skills and abilities on their own as they slowly find their way around the world and study their place within it. It's almost like empaths have this superpower of adaptability. They observe that around them, swish it around, and end up with a better understanding and control over what they do from there. It's like playing with clay and reshaping the clump as you go along. Empaths, it seems, just know how to shape the clay the right way.

However, this process isn't enough to develop all their abilities and reach their full potential. That's where personal awareness, hard work, willingness, and effort come into play. When doing so, an empath can make a difference to those around them and the world.

How to Get Where You Want to Go

You're a delicately and accurately constructed and mapped out work of art, chiseled and scraped to form all your abilities, skills, traits, quirks, and everything else that makes you uniquely who you are: true nature, they call it. However, you can call it whatever you want; it doesn't change what it is and how you can't run from what life has waiting for you behind the big, bold doors of what and who you were meant to be.

There's a great inevitability of being unable to change your fate, so why even try? Most empaths go through life without identifying as one, ashamed of their gifts and capabilities, and working their hardest to suppress and run away from the persons they are. Life's already hard enough as it is without adding distinct views, outlooks, experiences, and unique abilities. Empaths, as you know, must deal with all that while also taking in pimples, blemishes, growth pains, hormones, professions, and all. That which sets them apart from the crowds might be the thing that causes them to deny their true selves. No one wants to feel different, weird or alienated from their peers, after all. So I'll give it to you straight: Empaths aren't your everyday, run-of-the-mill people. They are, without a doubt, different. However, no one ever said that it was a bad thing.

However, a distant relative known as human nature often steps in the way. We're usually led to believe that we need to be accepted and liked by everyone, that the opinions of others are what defy us, and that without a group or clique, we aren't living our best lives.

We're all just shape-sorters in that we want to fit somewhere and would do almost anything to find the right shape to match our own. We wish to belong—it's as simple as that. It's not anyone's fault; it's just how we've been programmed by our histories and societies.

Yet, the fact stands: There's no point fighting something with no tactics, strategies, or victories. True nature doesn't have a switch or plug to pull. You can't run from it, and even when you try, you'll find that you never get what you truly want out of life, simply because your matching shape is one of a kind; one that isn't on the shape sorter itself.

Only when you learn to accept and embrace that will you be able to take that leap forward in life and find the person you really are and what you have to offer the world. First, you have to accept that you're an empath and are different. Then, you must come to terms with the fact that it's nothing short of a gift embedded deep within your true nature, and it's here to stay. It's the first step you have to take before you can channel, develop, strengthen, and perfect the innate powers and abilities within you. Only then will you be able to find your perfect fit in life and move on to the other ways in which you can activate your powers as an empath.

Throughout the previous chapters, we've discussed what it means to be an empath, sure signs and traits you have, some pros and cons, and the whole deal. We've learned quite a lot, and plenty of information will still come your way. However, since we're now working on how to enhance and train your abilities, it's important to remember your aspirations, struggles, strengths, and all those delightful and often not-so-fun things that empaths have to deal with.

Remember to Look In

Being so involved and absorbed in others often means you forget to take a peek on the inside. However, if you do, you're often left with an intense feeling of guilt and remorse because you're not focusing your time, compassion, and efforts on those around you.

While I know your routine might be a bit busier than most, you must set aside time in your schedule dedicated to you and you alone. Focus the timeframe on recharging your energy reserve, loving yourself, and doing the things that bring you joy and peace.

Take time to listen to your emotions and thoughts, and embrace your sensitivities. Grab your gear and spend some time in nature or cuddle up at home with a good book or do some arts and crafts. Pamper yourself with a good self-care routine, wholesome snacks, or relaxation techniques. Take a few good breaths and meditate whenever you get the chance! Which, luckily for you, is easy to do considering all the guided meditation scripts coupled into every chapter.

Strictly Precautionary

As you know by now, empaths are individuals that lead with their gut and have a problem with marking off limits and establishing personal parameters. Hence, the key lies in learning to trust your intuition, setting boundaries, and grabbing the ropes of your empathic abilities.

Intuition: The first rule in mastering your intuitive abilities is learning to trust yourself, the messages you receive, and those hunches you get from time to time. Next, focus on connecting to life, your surroundings, feelings, and specific situations to strengthen that gut feeling and pick up on things quickly when they come around. So, listen, trust, and believe that little voice inside your head, and know that intuition just knows best.

Boundaries: With some help from intuition, you'll be able to spot all those energy vampires and "fakes" that drain and bruise you from a mile away! However, you can't dodge them all, right? This is especially when and why you need some sturdy, steadfast boundaries and borders set in place. Setting clear boundaries for yourself and those around you will allow you to distance yourself from those who wish you harm or unwillingly cause you stress. It can be as simple as saying that your me-time can't be interrupted or asking to stick to specific talking points. Whatever the walls, set them up and maintain them throughout your life. Remember that it's not selfish; it's a way of protecting yourself. Those who genuinely care for you will find the understanding and acceptance to respect where you're coming from.

Knowing the ropes: The biggest and most well-known empathic ability is that you can feel, comprehend, mirror, and heal the feelings, emotions, and energies of those around you. Although it slips off the tongue, it also means that you have to suck up all the negativity that floods the world around you. I know it's a tedious part of the gig, but still a part of the job, nonetheless. However, there are ways in which you can transmute these energies and turn the negatives upside down. Start each day with positive affirmations and mantras, surround yourself with succulents or crystals, and have a good laugh whenever things get dark and gloomy. Negativity is a powerful energy, but it doesn't have to be the controlling force in your life, especially when you know how to bend it in real time. All it takes is a bit of practice and some good aids. Positivity is much more flattering, after all.

Last call: Last but not least, be grateful for your gift. You're a particular person, and once you accept all you are, you can take the world by storm and develop your abilities more and more by the day. Gratitude goes a long way, so open yourself up freely and consciously to the world of an empath, challenge yourself where you can, know your self-worth, and remember that you're a real-life superhero; all that's left is the cape!

White Light Meditation

Meditation, and all the different kinds you get, can often seem like an unfamiliar ball in your garage. However, all it takes are a few minutes each day, and it will get easier from there on out. Soon you'll barely be able to recall a time where you weren't breathing, visualizing, and connecting with your inner peace. Meditation is the stepping stone in unlocking your abilities and learning to live and accept the person you are and the true nature you've been hiding away. It's time to connect and reshape the way you see your gifts.

Step One:

Find a quiet place that makes it easy for you to stay concentrated, comfortable, and at peace. If there are distractions, noises, and people, it might not be best to plop down in the middle of it all. You need your time alone, and things like that will only get in the way of the process. If you enjoy nature, for example, you can pick an area outside, but if you feel that the grass might cause you to itch, perhaps take up a space indoors. The choice is, however, as always, only yours to make.

Once you're comfortable, lay down flat on the ground, keeping your body straight, with one arm at your side and the other on your solar plexus chakra, located right below your chest and above your belly. Make sure to keep your body loose and limber, without tension, and fully relaxed, almost as if you're just about to take a nap, or you've just barely woken up.

Choosing your posture wisely will make it much easier for you to get comfortable before meditation and stay that way throughout, while possibly opening up the freedom of your other chakras. Then, once you're in a tranquil spot and laid to rest (without death), you can begin with letting the light in. However, before you get to that, there's still a step or two you'll have to do, and it all starts with taking a breath.

Step Two:

As you're lying on the ground, close your eyes and shift your focus onto your breathing patterns, taking deep and long breaths that help you relax and remove stress from the body. Try imagining your breaths blowing away your problems, thoughts, and the plans you have later, and feel yourself become present with your meditation and nothing else. As you're breathing, try using your diaphragm to fill your lungs, and as you're breathing out, push out the air and deflate your stomach as you do so. Proper breathing is a key to truly reaping the benefits of your grounding techniques. Focus only on your breathing, and truly sink into your body, environment, and zen state of mind. Continue breathing for a few minutes, and whenever you're ready, slowly move onto the next step.

Step Three:

As you're breathing, slowly open the gates of the universe, the palms of healing hands, or whatever imagery resonates with you the most, and picture a bright light leaking out toward you.

See the path it travels, the waves or straight line it takes, the warmth of it as it nears. See the light and envision it crawling closer. Take notice of it entering the crown of your head. Follow it as it expands throughout your body, penetrating and purifying each limb. Guide it throughout your body until all you can see is the light, and all you can feel is its warmth. Allow yourself to sit with this light and focus on how it flickers as you breathe and how it makes you feel.

Hold the image for a few moments, or for as long as you like. Simply sit, admire, and allow the thoughts and feelings to come to you. Whenever you're ready, allow the light to leave your body, slowly and gently. Return to the presence, taking deep breaths as you ground yourself to reality, and open your eyes. You can get up or stay there for a while, until you're ready to get back to your day and shine your own light out to the world.

What's Next?

Knowing what you can do as an empath, and how to make it your superpower, will help you embrace your identity, authentic self, and abilities to change the world for the better. From here on out, you can proceed to the next steps of learning more about your specific gifts and how you can develop them and truly discover the art of awareness, acceptance, and empathic greatness.

Chapter 4:
Intuition

"Thank you, Franklin. I'm here in Yellow Springs, where a five-year-old boy has been missing since early this morning after camping with his family south of the small village. As you can see behind me, the village's people have grouped together in hopes of finding the boy before sunset, as the wind grows unkind, and his parents, along with everyone else, grow more concerned. However, we remain optimistic. All we can do now is hope that the boy will be found unscathed, unharmed, and that he will be returned safely to his home in no time..."

Anne Bromberick stared at her TV, biting her nails as she waited to hear some good news regarding the young boy's disappearance. There were none; no clues, leads, or idea where he had gone.

It was a tragic event that had transpired in their small village, and as she had moved away years ago and could not join the search party, all she could do was sit and wait. It crushed her, but still she sat and waited for hours on end.

Then, finally, a buzz goes off next to her, lighting up the screen with a reply from her mother: "Your father and brother are out looking for him. The search parties are hopeful. However, it's getting late, and we fear a storm might come in. His poor parents are worried sick, of course. I'll keep you updated if I hear anything on my end, dear."

Groaning, she stood up, pacing around on the carpet. Anne decided that she couldn't just sit around anymore, waiting for luck to come around. There wasn't any time to waste, the boy needed help, and if anyone could give him that, or at least try, it would be her. She ran to her backyard and sat in the grass. It had been years since she used her empathic abilities, and she was unsure she'd be able to pull it off this time. However, she knew that it wasn't a choice or debate; she had to do whatever it took, as the little boy's life was on the line.

I have to focus, clear my mind, and breathe, she thought, taking deep breaths through her nose and blowing them out with a loud whoosh. Think about him, focus on him...

The wind slowly brushed her skin and curled through her hair, the grass tickling her calves, and the soft setting sun kissed her hairline.

"Breathe," she whispered, allowing herself to be grounded in the world and enter a different state of mind, pinpointing energies in search of the one that belonged to the young boy. The grass softened around her, and her body dropped into herself.

And then it happened: Her teeth chattered loudly and her skin got coated in layers of goosebumps as she shivered at the sudden drop in temperatures. She felt chilled to the bone, and the damp sensation on her legs didn't do her any favors. She noted a strong scent of unturned soil, and the sweet, pungent zest of approaching rain.

It's him! she thought. It has to be.

She saw fragmentary glimpses of shrubbery, a large tree trunk that was slightly hugging her from behind, wrapped up in vines and surrounded by falling pine cones. She pushed further, attempting to look around some more in hopes of finding some sort of landmark or clear indication of the boy's surroundings, anything that could act as a flare to where he was—anything would do.

That's when she heard it: The slight sound of water. A soft stream murmuring as it traveled along its bed, rippling over rocks, branches, and mud. It wasn't a large mass of water, but a big enough stream to make a sound. That's how they'll get to him.

She pulled herself back to reality, jumping up and rushing to her phone. With trembling hands, she called her father and told him what she had seen. Her father was a hunter, always had been, and since he had been trailing the area since he was a child, he knew the woods like the back of his hands.

With Anne's description, he was able to paint a good idea of where the search had to go. It was a small, desolate area of the woods, and people barely made their way there at all. It was a good three miles from the campsite where the boy was last seen, so, of course, her father was hesitant. Nonetheless, he went, trusting his daughter's instincts. In her gut, she could feel that her visions wouldn't let them down and that she had sent the search party onto the right path. She knew he had to be there.

The line went quiet before cutting off entirely. Anne rushed to the TV and waited for any sign or signal of the boy's whereabouts. Anticipation and hopefulness danced clearly through the screen on both ends.

"Please, please be there," she whispered, her fingers inadvertently crossed as she waited to see the boy appear within the camera's view or any gesture of him to sound from the reporter's mouth. "Please, please..."

"We found him!"

Her heart skipped a beat as her father's voice echoed in the background. The reporter turned in shock. Anne jumped up, her tear-filled eyes glued to the scene. She laughed out of relief as she watched her father rush over to the medics with the boy wrapped in a blanket. The boy looked tired, scared, confused, and quiet as the camera crew crowded him. Yet, he was unscathed and in good shape.

The reporter mumbled a few things Anne neglected to catch as her eyes were fixed on the boy. He wants his parents, she thought. The reporter stuffed the mic in front of the boy's mouth. "I want a hotdog," he said. Okay, so perhaps her abilities needed some tuning...

Intuitive Empath: A Review

Throughout the book, I've used the term, *intuition*, frequently and told you to "trust your gut" indefinitely. Nonetheless, I thought giving the definition of intuition another go would make for a perfect start to this chapter.

Intuition is when we just know or understand things simply because we have a feeling about it. It ends up taking the place of logic and reason. It's that "feeling" that pops up from time to time and guides your decisions, choices, and feelings. A sixth sense of some sort. It's like when you can pick up on a kind face, when you know where something is, or when you just have an innate sense, feeling, or hunch about when things just don't feel right. It's about leading and leaning into your gut and trusting that it wants and knows the best for you, simply because intuition often does.

Intuitive empaths, on the other hand, have intuitions pushed to work in overdrive; they can spot and feel things that others can't. As well as outwardly demonstrating intuitive abilities toward those around them, they often feel senses of intuition toward situations on an inward level. So, they can spot "fakes" without thinking twice and know when they're mixed up in the right or wrong situations within a heartbeat.

They don't have to be told how others are feeling because deep down inside, they already know when someone's holding back, or when they're lying, if they're no good, or if they're solid. They can see past others without the curtain being pulled back because their guts are one of the best.

It's often said that all empaths are intuitive; however, sometimes, that's not the case: Some empaths have a strong intuition, while others' can use some work. You might have to do some further research and study before declaring your intuition as your most substantial empathic ability. I know it might sound confusing, but when you're an intuitive empath, I trust you'll know it.

Intuitive Traits

Seeing Points

Intuitive empaths can read and understand what others are feeling and where they're coming from. While all empaths have a greater understanding than most "normal" folk, intuitive empaths take a step up the ladder to really see why others are acting in specific ways, what their true intents are, and why they're feeling, thinking, or doing things in particular ways. They simply see points that are often harder for some to comprehend, and they even see those hidden from the naked eye.

Sensitivity and Energies

Intuitive empaths are especially attuned to the thoughts, emotions, and feelings of others, taking them in as their own while also dealing with their own internal struggles, as most empaths do. However, intuitive empaths might take up a more significant deal, but only because they can see and take on additional viewpoints and bits of information. As empaths, they hate seeing those around them suffer and would do anything to put a smile on their face. They hate negativity (as I hope everyone does). They prefer positive, uplifting, and radiant energies and environments. Luckily for them, intuitive empaths have an advantage where they can avoid seeing and running into bad things or taking the wrong turn into situations that'll leave them feeling gloomy, drained, or like they would've been better off staying at home.

Cramping Crowds

Intuitive empaths hate large groups and gatherings as much as the next empath does. Also, because they have this intensified overload of thoughts, emotions, and sensations, they're more likely to fall into a surplus of absorption, which can cause internal distress and drainage. It's a lot and most definitely something no one wants. Not only can it take a knock on their emotional and mental state, but it can lead to a multitude of physical aches and ailments, such as migraines and fatigue.

Open Eyes and Clearer Skies

Empaths are notorious for their ability to detect and embody the feelings, thoughts, and circumstances of those around them. However, these abilities often come without the user manual. They don't get post-its, instructions, and notes on why people feel the way they do or whether they're feeling their own emotions or those of others. It can be confusing, for sure, and who can blame them? But that's where intuitive empaths have the upper hand: They can take a step back to look at the broader picture behind people, seeing emotions, causes, effects, and all they need to finally set up the final peek. Their insight and understanding are like no other and it lives with them, rent-free! Intuitive empaths are also very in tune with themselves and their inner state, allowing them to differentiate between their own emotions and experiences and those of others. I don't know why or how, but it seems that they're better (or at least find it easier) to set up the necessary boundaries and barriers to draw the line between someone else and themself.

Help in Understanding

Intuitive empaths have a more remarkable ability to understand what others are trying to tell them. At the same time, they can discuss the emotions, thoughts, dreams, and worries of others more clearly, all the while listening through and through. They can intuitively perceive and understand why others are feeling specific ways, guiding them where they're hesitant, and helping clear up the bigger picture they want to grasp. That's why intuitive empaths make great counselors and advice-givers. In addition, they're creative, as most empaths are, with a knack for thinking outside the box, solving problems, and keeping their minds open to various solutions, possibilities, and views. They're also known to be walking lie detectors. Intuitive empaths run on their gut feel and instincts, meaning that it's nearly impossible to lie to them or hide anything away, so if you were thinking of telling an intuitive empath "I'm fine" when you're not, think again.

Furthermore, intuitive empaths are laced with other knacks and ticks that make them unique in their empathic type and abilities. They're a rare few, and if you're one of them, you should consider yourself lucky! You can read people like an open book, which allows you to heal, care, listen, know, and respond. So, if that's you, why don't you get to reading!

Developing Powers

Intuition lives inside all of us; whether we choose to listen to our guts or that tiny voice in the back of our heads is another thing. Intuitive empaths have these intuitions that work overtime and are simply better at getting the job done. Yet, not all intuitive empaths know the ins and outs of listening, decoding, and trusting their intuitive skills. Sometimes, whether it's a gift or not, things need some polishing and development before they can function the way they should, or better. However, intuition is something we all have (even when it comes off as lousy), and if you're an empath, you can be more than one type. Therefore, if you've found yourself plucking a lot more rotten fruit than ripe ones, you're often at the wrong place at the wrong time, or you "just don't know" things, you can rest assured that your intuition can be sharpened, grown, and improved. All you have to do is put in the work and effort, and you'll be catching hunches and bad people in no time. So, how do you develop your intuitive powers?

Rotating Routines

How we live our lives with specific routines and habits takes a significant toll on how we use our abilities. A healthy body and mind call for healthier functioning and power utilization, correct? Well, that's what I'm suggesting. Our minds and bodies are robust systems that need to be taken care of. A dusty, rusted computer won't work well, after all, so why would our bodies if we neglect and abuse them day after day? Hence, the first step in developing your empathic and intuitive abilities and powers is looking into your life, habits, and patterns to see whether it's up to par. After that, it's all about taking your life by the horns, brushing off the dust catchers, cleaning the components, and fixing up the dents and cracks, before finally switching on your intuition for the long run.

Keeping Health

As with most things in life, there has to be a balance for things to work as they should. Your body and mind are no different, and for you to sharpen your intuitive abilities, you'll have to find a balance in your life and keep your mental and physical health in tip-top shape.

As they say, the early bird gets the worm. In this case, the bird will be the only one to catch it simply because it has intuition on its side. When waking up early, you open up time in your schedule and gain more out of life. Why not take that extra time to revitalize your energy, boost your intuitive abilities, or simply catch up on some hobbies? However, that doesn't mean you should skimp on how long you sleep. Ensure you're getting the right amount of snooze time to keep your health polished in all departments.

To further keep yourself in a balanced light you'll have to go back to the basics: eating right, working out, drinking water, breathing properly, and keeping your noggin clean and clear.

Since childhood, we were told, whether it was by our parents, guardians, teachers, or doctors, that we need to be mindful of what we put on our plates. "Not too many sweetmeats," "remember the veggies," and all that stuff we didn't want to hear back then. I mean, sometimes we hate hearing it now! Look, you don't have to tell me about how a good comfort meal can make the day, but in the long run, having a greasy patty over that chicken salad simply won't stick.

Proper eating is the first step in nurturing the body, keeping it healthy, and holding on to wholesome habits and routines that'll make your empathic abilities easier to reach.

Try slacking on your sugars, alcohols, caffeines, and any other inflammatory foods and drinks, as they keep you from tapping into your intuition. I'm not saying you should ditch these batches in a single sitting; small steps will suffice. However, eliminating, or at least decreasing, these groups would do you good. So, why not follow your intuition on this one? Not your wants, cravings, or heart, your intuition, because deep down, I think you know it's the right fork to pick.

And don't forget to drink enough water! It's an essential part of life and being alive. You also need it to regulate your emotions, neutralize your energy, and kick away any migraines or other physical pains. Furthermore, clear water calls for clear intuition, and without it your inner guidance will be way off. So, ensure you're getting enough H_2O!

Your doctor would further say to get in your minutes of sweating, and they're not wrong. Exercising is an excellent boost of energy that'll keep you balanced in life, while also helping you cocoon onto and better understand the information you receive from others.

Then we have the mind, which can be taken care of in various ways: breathing properly, meditating, silence or awareness exercises, journaling, or simply cutting yourself some slack from time to time. The mind is an essential component in psychic communication and empathic ability development. Looking after it will ensure you take in all the power it offers, while being able to work clearly with your intuition. Nobody wants to "power up" with a fogged-up or clotted mind. Therefore, you have to keep it in the best shape it could be, especially since yours is prone to overheating and getting blocked with all the things around you. Look after your mind, that's all I'm saying, and your gut feel will follow.

Above all else, remember to keep an ear out for what your body and energy is telling you. There are no amount of self-help books, motivational seminars, or workshops that can know you better than you know yourself. Don't jump or sprint simply because some coach or article said so. You know what works and what doesn't work for your energy and how your body responds to different things. Listen to yourself and your needs. If you feel that certain activity levels are too strenuous or that you can't start off with 40 minutes per day, then don't. Cut down the time or intensity by only running for five minutes and pushing weights every other day. Making small lifestyle changes is a start and more than enough to get you healthed up.

Lastly, learn to trust your intuition as it is. Tap into your energies and intuition and recognize them when they come up in your day-to-day. Try keeping tabs on these moments by jotting them down. It can help you gain awareness of your intuitive abilities while showing you that, no matter how big or small, your intuition has been there all along, guiding you through your life.

Test yourself by trying to predict what's going to happen short term and see how many times you were correct. Build confidence and believe in yourself and in your intuition, even when you have a couple of slips, hiccups, and moments of utter failure. Nothing happens overnight, and nothing can be flawless, so don't get discouraged when things don't go as planned. All it takes is learning to work with your gut and not against it, and trusting that your intuition is here to stay.

Sorting Through

Take a look around you: What do you see? How many things are there? Is there clutter? Things you haven't used in decades? Take a good look. Everything you see, whether alive or not, has an energy to it. So, if you find that you're prone to hoarding, overcrowding yourself with things, or just a *Material Girl* (or boy), you might want to know that you're setting up a physical barrier weighing you down at this very moment. A simple day of spring cleaning and decluttering can do wonders, whether it be your workspace, whole home, or a single room. Once you've got everything sorted through and cleaned out, you'll have a more precise, lighter, and greater flow of thought and, in turn, intuition. Your house will also reap some benefits from that.

Decluttering and tidying up isn't limited to clearing out the physical spaces around you. It's about giving your whole life a nice scrub and looking at your everyday schedule, tasks, habits, and even those you surround yourself with. Everything that isn't good for you and your energy must go. So, be honest and open about what's holding your intuition and well-being down, before moving past them.

Look at how you spend your hours and whether you're overloading yourself with information and tasks. If you, for example, find yourself constantly glued to your screen, try cutting back time with the cords and instead go for an intuition or meditation class. It's all about awareness and consideration for yourself.

Simply take some time to summarize what's going on in your life and what has to change. Then, ask yourself for some inner guidance, reassess your dreams and beliefs, establish boundaries, and connect with others while remaining deliberate about the people you plan on keeping around.

You have to be ready and willing to make these changes. You can't expect things to be different all on their own, after all. There has to be a push, shove, or even a simple nudge to do the job. The point is, there's a reason intuition isn't knocking at the door every time you stumble across sketchy deals; it's blocked, and only when you remove the block will you and your intuition be able to see steadily. Assess, release, and move on, as better days of "knowing" are ahead.

Just Let It Happen

I can tell you all about meditation and intuition exercises; however, it won't do you any good if you're not in it to win it. At the end of the day, working on your empathic and intuitive abilities is all up to you. You need to put yourself out there, pay attention to your surroundings, let your thoughts and feelings be known, and live life with your gut in your back pocket at all times. Trusting yourself and knowing that you're capable of anything is the ultimate step to take—once you do that, you'll be just fine! So, live easily, take a break, be creative, dance without the music, and listen to the signs intuition throws your way.

Tuning In

When we hear *meditation*, we often see images of people sitting with their legs folded, peaceful as they *oom* and *aam* on a yoga mat. For some, it might be an accurate description, and there's nothing wrong with that. Whether you're a mat person or not, meditation in all forms is a great way to destress and pull the weight of the day from your shoulders. It's a way of calming and opening your mind while switching to your subconscious thinking. Since we're often prone to blocking ourselves from our intuition (even when involuntary), we need to find ways to unblock and tune into a state of mind that allows it to shine through. The main ingredient is simply finding peace within yourself and forgetting what holds you back.

Trying Trataka

Step One:

Sit or lie in a quiet, safe, and comfortable area, as you've done before. Make sure you have a candle and a lighter or some matches ready on the side. We'll get to that in a minute. For now, only focus on ensuring you're comfortable and that your candle is somewhere reachable and sturdy (we don't want a fire on our hands).

Step Two:

Slowly start tuning into your consciousness by focusing on your third eye, located between your eyebrows and the centermost part of the brain. It's essential to deepen and keep your focus here as it's your intuitive and clairvoyant chakra. If your mind wanders, simply shift your focus back onto the spot. Take a few deep breaths as you're doing so.

Step Three:

You can now light the candle in front of you. Keep it lit as you close your eyes again, taking three deep breaths to completely rest and relax your body, and recenter your thoughts onto your third eye.

Step Four:

Open your eyes and gaze at the flame, trying not to blink and keeping your gaze set. Once your eyes start to burn and water, close them again, before focusing on the image of the candle and flame in your third eye. Look upward and inward. When the image fades, gaze at the candle again, keeping your gaze until they burn again. Repeat as many times as you deem fit.

Step Five:

When you're ready to finish up, cup your hands over your closed eyes and look down before gently opening them to look at the void for a few minutes before ending the session with a few deep breaths to resettle yourself into reality.

What's Next?

We often hear the phrase "trust your gut," and in my case, I happen to say it a lot. For empaths, this holds true more than for others. In trusting your intuition, you can learn to trust yourself, your abilities, and the messages you receive through your other capabilities. Some might say that intuition makes you move, and boy isn't that true!

Important note before we move forward!

Research shows that people who help others (with zero expectations) experience higher levels of fulfillment, live longer, and are more in control of their lives.

I would like to create the opportunity to deliver this value to you during your reading experience. To do so, I have a simple question for you:

<u>Would you help someone you've never met if it didn't cost you money?</u>

<u>But you never received credit for it?</u>

If so, I have an "ask" to make on behalf of someone you don't know and likely never will.

They are just like you, or like you were a few years ago: They seek information but are unsure where to look because they are less experienced and have a strong desire to help the world...

This is where you come in.

Most people do the same thing: they judge a book by its cover (and its reviews). And the only way for me, as an author, to accomplish my mission of helping as many empaths as possible is by reaching them.

If you have found this book valuable thus far, please, take a brief moment to give an honest review of the book and its content!

It will cost you zero dollars and take less than 60 seconds. Your review will help... one more empath break free from this overwhelm that makes our lives hard and live a meaningful life. One more life change for the betterment of humanity...

Use your next 60 seconds to make that happen, and leave a review!

Click here if you bought the ebook: https://geni.us/empathsebook

Scan here if you bought the paperback:

Just scroll down the page and find this option:

Thank you!

Review this product

Share your thoughts with other customers

Write a customer review

Chapter 5:
Aura Reading

It was still early in the morning, and as expected, the airport was still uneventful and tranquil. Only a few people loitered, waiting for their early morning flights. Yet still, there was a sense of haste and activity in the air. It was among the humming atmosphere that a true-blue empath walked, aptly named Iris. Although, at this moment, she didn't yet know of her ability.

She was waiting at one of the large windows, staring out at the runways, airplanes, and tarmac workers. She had booked her flight months ago, but had only realized her mistake that week. She wanted to change it, since she was anything but a morning person, but something had stopped her: a feeling that she had to leave the ticket as is. She had no idea why she had that feeling or what it meant, but somehow she just knew it was the thing to do. So, that's why she was here at two in the morning, waiting for a flight that was scheduled to take off at three.

The flight was for Seattle, and within Seattle was an art gallery. It was a pop-up exhibition rumored to feature some of her favorite artists and photographers. That's what she was: A photographer who sometimes dappled in paint. She treasured colors and felt something more whenever she saw them.

Even when her eyes grew heavier and her body started to slump, she couldn't control the excitement flourishing inside. A smile never left her face. Her fingers slowly played with the strap of her camera bag, rubbing the braided stitches as she glanced at the clock. Any minute now, she thought, heartbeat starting to race. A week with nothing but colors! she thought, reciting the schedule she had laid out: galleries, museums, walks in the parks and streets—all of it.

Her gaze returned to the outside, where she saw two men: airline baggage handlers, having a good laugh. Even without hearing their contagious laughter, the silent conversation brought her joy. It was pure bliss shared between two people, something you rarely see that raw. She wanted to capture it.

So, she pulled her camera from its beige holder almost instinctively. (I know what you're thinking: "Privacy!" But it's not illegal. And she means well.) She pulled the viewfinder up to her face, squinting her eyes as she always did. And with a click, the photo was taken. Smiling, she took a moment to admire the scene once again, before looking down at the picture. She frowned. The image on the display wasn't of the two men, or anything at all, for that matter. It was an image of its own, one of blurred colors mingled up, yet still they held a light. Vivid green, light pink, golden yellow, and hints of navy blue and putrid green.

She turned the camera to look over at the lens. After not seeing anything, she wiped it off softly. Perhaps, something was in front of it? she guessed. She looked up at the men as they stubbed out their cigarettes and walked away. She sighed, knowing that moment couldn't be recaptured, and that it was lost for good.

Still, when looking back down at the image, there was a feeling of sense and reasoning that only she could understand. Just in case, and to confirm her suspicions, she pulled the camera up to see whether there was some kind of glare or something that had caused the image to turn out that way—nothing. She took another photo, and it came out clear. She decided to let it go, but that gnawing feeling was still stuck in the pit of her chest. She moved over to the colored image again. This time a smile crept onto her face as she thought of the perfect name to match the sketch:

"Aura."

What Is an Aura?

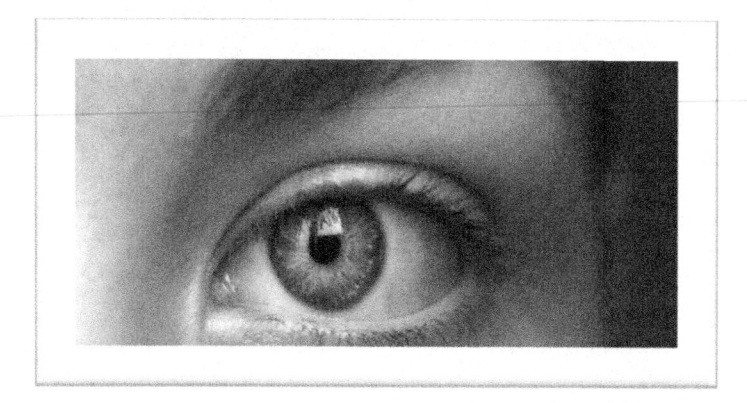

Auras are like bubbles perfectly blown to fit and surround every individual being and thing, outlined with pinks, yellows, blues, and greens. They're often referred to as the color of emotion simply because that's what they are: your feelings, experiences, and energies displayed through bursts of color.

Sometimes, the best way to describe something is by using a picture that makes no sense. So, here it is: We're all just a bunch of oranges shifting around on plates. Yes, I know it might sound strange, but hear me out.

Take the image below: it's a simple half-cut orange resting on two plates (even though it's one, just pretend), one white, the other blue. Each color represents different meanings, which we'll get to in a moment. So, what does this have to do with auras and energies, you ask. Well, I might be walking a wide circle here, but just like how the plates line the orange, our auras surround us, encircling us with colors. Whenever we shift to different surroundings, emotions, or stages in our lives, we take the plates, wash them up, and get different colors in their place.

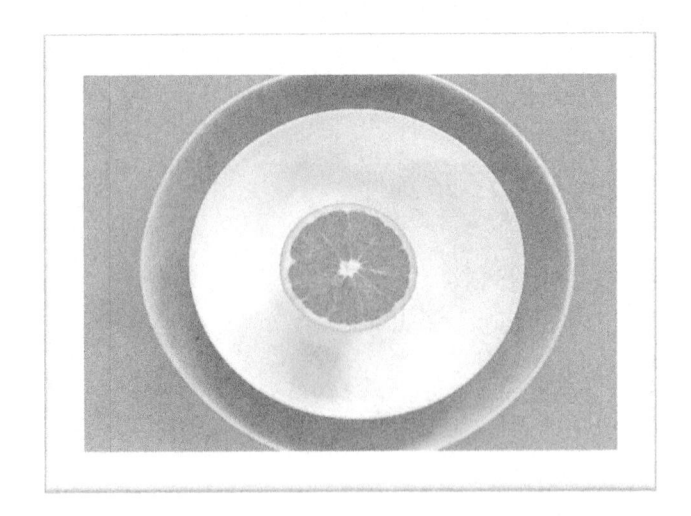

For the sake of the metaphor and imagery, imagine that the two plates perfectly matched the color of the background. It would make it pretty hard or impossible to see, wouldn't it? Well, this is, to some degree, how auras work. Most people can't see them, with the exception of the gifted view. However, if you were to tap your hand next to the fruit, you would still feel the plates. In the same way, almost everyone can feel auras, in that they can sense them.

Pigmentation Explanation

Every person's aura has different layers and colors, although there's usually a primary color people latch onto—except for the multicolored few. Nonetheless, whether you're holding onto more hue than most or you're shining through single digits, the meaning behind the colors remains the same: They're all associated with different types of energies and personalities.

If you're not particularly happy with the color of your aura, don't worry! You're not stuck with a single one for the rest of your life. In fact, it changes relatively often, and not only throughout your life, but in a single day. Your aura vibrations, as explained, are caused by your emotions, thoughts, and situations, making it easy to shift and tilt as you move between energies. In short, your aura simply hops along for the ride, changing whenever you progress in life, experience setbacks, and when you're just going about your day. So, let's get to the color wheel of aura meanings:

- When thinking of the associations made with red, you might see glimpses of throbbing hearts, and passionate gestures. Then again, perhaps you see bursts of hate, ego, and resentment. Either way, you wouldn't be wrong. The red aura can come in brighter or darker shades. The former represents lighter and more positive energies, with sensuality, compassion, courage, and creativity on its side. The latter, however, leans to the darker side, showcasing negativity, anger, trauma, and violence.
- If you think about it, pink is merely a light shade of red. Therefore, you could've guessed that its meaning is very similar. It represents love and softness of all sorts, like the love between a parent and child, that naive first love, an unconditional love surrounded by softness, peace, sincerity, tenderness, and harmony. Perhaps, that's why Valentine's Day and pink often go hand in hand.
- Within the darker hues of purple lies magic, intuition, nobility, visionary qualities, wisdom, and spirituality. This is usually where your empaths come into play. Still, their auras can change color without them losing their empathic natures.
- Magenta, part of the pink-red-and-purple family, holds an individuality of its own. Its creativity, humor, and teeny bits of weirdness, combined with spirituality and love is a unique aura that simply demands attention from time to time.
- In times when you're at ease, courageous, friendly, ambitious, comfortable in your own skin, and within a varied social setting, you better bet you're shining orange and beyond! It's an aura often showcasing maturity, vigor, energy, and an optimism that only an unspoken confidence can quietly demand.
- When it comes to the yellows, there's a brighter side and one that's purely golden. While you might not believe it at first,

the brightest aura might not be the best as they usually indicate immaturity, naivety, self-centeredness, and self-absorption. However, the golden ones have healthy, happy, easy-going, and flowing shines that are intelligent, optimistic, and free, just like the sun.
- Green is the color of nature and of life and growth. Therefore, it's not a big stretch to take it up as an aura of health, healing and transformation. Then again, when the green gets less vivid and more putrid, your aura could mean illness, disease, envy, or lacking a sense of energy or balance.
- When it comes to blue, you have to have your lighter hue, as well as some navies. That's exactly what you have when looking at the sky-like auras. Both, however, have a related meaning in that they represent the intellectual, analytical, and logical mind. Both wouldn't mind cashing some checks and pulling in some dough.
- Another family of the blues, indigo showcases a lighter personality than his distant cousin. Indigo auras involves being more on the right-minded side and keeping to themselves. It beams intuition, curiosity, and a search for honesty.
- Brown auras are often in need of help. It could scream toward a lost soul who has strayed off the path toward addiction and self-sabotage. They need a direction that they struggle to find. However, another reason someone might be showcasing a bit more tan than usual might be that they're grounded, career-driven, and ready to get their hands busy with some tasks.

While auras aren't limited to these colors alone, and there is still plenty to learn about them, I think the basics of what the colors of emotions mean have been covered. Sometimes, you just need to focus on what you're seeing, whether it's on yourself or others. Appreciate the colors you see, step in when things look hazy or wrong, and see colors not for what they look like but for what they are.

What Happens in an Aura Reading?

I can blabber on and on about auras as much as I want. However, when it comes to having your aura read, I think it's better if we get down to the steps:

1. In traditional aura readings, the aura reader will direct you to a comfortable, usually quiet place where both of you are undisturbed.
2. The reader will then take 15 minutes to half an hour to thoroughly take in and understand your aura: its shades, colors, textures, and whether it requires any cleaning up or healing on the side.
3. After they've gathered a summary, they'll share their findings with you. They'll discuss what your colors mean, where you have imbalances within your energy, areas of concern, and methods of cleansing and healing your aura.

Snapshots

If you're more into things that aren't too traditional, an aura reading with cameras and polaroids might be for you. Here's what you can expect:

1. In an aura photography reading, you'll find yourself in a geode tent, sitting with your hands on two sensors that are able to read electromagnetic energies.
2. You'll be facing the camera for a bit as you wait for the double exposure and overall film to develop. Once that's over, you'll sit down for your reading.
3. Just as with a traditional reading, you'll be given your colors and what they represent and mean in your life, while getting some hints and suggestions of what you should do next. The only difference is that they get their information from the image, and you have something physical to see for yourself.

Reading Auras

When it comes to reading the auras of others and of yourself, there's nothing that a bit of guidelines can't help with, and that's precisely what I have here for you today.

Before the Read

As with most things that are harder to touch and see, developing the ability to view and read auras takes time and effort. However, you have to first step into the right state of mind.

Clearing your mind, whether through sessions of meditation, mindfulness exercises, or simply taking a deep breath, is an essential part of getting into the right mindset and environment needed to open yourself up to seeing and reading auras properly.

How to See

Auras are fragile things when you think about it, and you won't be able to see them at all if you go in guns blazing, roughly, or anything like that. Coupled within the intricacy that is aura reading lies the need for delicacy and attentiveness. The best way to take this on is shifting your view of the world, changing your peripheral vision, and softening your gaze. Here's one method to do so:

- You know how when looking at a candle you see this slight "smudge" of color surrounding the flame? Well, it's sort of what you're after when trying to spot auras: a smudge of color outlining the body. Still, where to start and how to fix your eyesight to better see those smears?
    - After taking a few good breaths, place one of your hands in front of a white or black surface within natural lighting.

- Focus on the space just above your middle finger, but don't look past your finger. The background should seem blurry. Do you see something?
- It's a method of defocusing that allows you to see that smudge of white, off-white, or yellow haze we're after. This is your aura.
- Once your vision is adjusted, you might be able to see multiple layers beaming from your aura, but it's not promised.

However, this method might not work for everyone. You might have to start off with a different technique, such as concentrating on your finger for a minute, looking away, and viewing your aura through your mind's eye, at least just until you grow more accustomed to seeing it with your physical eye.

In Pursuit of Color

Practice makes perfect, as they say. So, the best way to develop your abilities in aura reading would be to grab a friend or a mirror and work on seeing auras in real-time as much as possible. When asking a friend, it will work the same as it did with your hand, more or less. Simply do this:

- Take a few minutes with the person you're reading to clear both of your minds through a meditation or a breathing session. Get relaxed and comfortable so that nothing is blocking the person's aura, your reading, or making things harder than they should be.
- Let the person stand 10 feet away from you against a white or black background within natural lighting. The more natural the lighting, the better, but if you're experiencing some technical hitches, feel free to improvise.
- When ready, focus on their nose. Remember not to overfocus your gaze and to keep it relaxed and concentrated on your peripheral view.

- A gray shadow-like outline will start to form. It won't have a thick, in-your-face design. Instead, it'll hold a softer, more modest approach. However, when it comes, try not to stray from your focal point. I know it's exciting, but still, try to relax and stay concentrated.
- Observe the outline using only your peripherals. As you're doing this, the aura will slowly start to actualize before your eyes. Gently roll your gaze upward to their forehead, as to allow yourself a better glimpse of their aura. Don't get discouraged if you only see a single color within their aura; seeing multiple layers might not come straight out of the gate for everyone and could take numerous tries.
- If possible, try reading the same person's aura more than once, or your own (by using a mirror or your hands) more and more. Jot down your findings in a journal so that you can see your ability working and growing, and view the changes within colors, people, and yourself.

You must know that reading auras is no one-and-done, do-this-and-that thing; it's hard and requires practice, concentration, patience, commitment, and more. It can be especially frustrating at the start. When you blink, for example, you might see the aura disappear. It's a bummer, I know, but it happens. Blame your brain. Yet, as time and practice go by, it will happen less frequently. However, that's only one problem you might come across.

Reading someone's aura (or your own) can take days, weeks, months, or years before you hit the nail on the head and gather up the right amount of focus and channeling of self and consciousness. Then again, you never know, you might just get it right on your first try. The chances are 50/50 on this one.

Healing Auras

Your aura is your unspoken introduction to the world, the first point of contact that stretches beyond words and movements. It's much more than a simple coat of energy you throw on when the weather gets chilly; aura is all of you and nothing less. Therefore, looking after it is of utmost importance. When you feel your aura is bruised, there is a way of healing. Although straying away from traditional ways of meditation, this healing method allows you to work from the top and through, aura and out.

The Steps of Restoring

Step 1:

Before we start, take a seat somewhere quiet, and where you're comfortable and focused. Clear your mind and relax into yourself by taking a few deep breaths until you feel you're ready to start. Take your time.

Step 2:

Now, while being delicate with yourself and trusting your senses, try pinpointing the location of your aura. Continue breathing as you search around. Once you have it, try and see how far your aura extends outside of your body by imagining it expanding and contracting as you continue breathing. Don't force the radius, let it happen on its own terms and expand to where it's most comfortable. You might be able to visualize your aura or only sense it, but trust whichever comes your way. Think about what you're seeing or sensing and how it makes you feel: Joyous? Overwhelmed? Anything else? Simply take note of these thoughts, keep your eyes closed, and breathe.

Step 3:

Return your thoughts to your aura, and run through it, searching for any injuries, whether it be holes, tears, scarring, blemishes—anything. For now, simply take note of these wounds, taking in what you see, which injuries you have, and how many there are of each.

Step 4:

When you're ready, turn your focus back onto your injuries, this time taking it one at a time. For every individual mark, ask yourself this: When and how did it get there? Why am I holding onto it? How does it make me feel? Am I willing and ready to let it go? Take in and be open to all the emotions, thoughts, and information you're feeling and receiving. Trust your gut, remember? I know it might be hard at first, but simply trust that you're okay, that you know best, and that it's for the best. Praise yourself for your cooperation and self-awareness.

Step 5:

Shift your focus, once again, back onto your aura and injuries, this time seeing them heal and fade away. Imagine the dark spots and scar tissue softening away, the holes being refilled, the tears and slits stitching themselves up. Remember that it's not a race and to take your time. If you find yourself remembering things and reliving moments, allow yourself to feel, understand, and acknowledge them before letting them rest away with the injuries and marks. Continue healing your aura until it grows consistent all the way through, and you feel at ease with your energy. Remember to breathe, and whenever you're ready to do so, simply open your eyes.

What's Next?

Auras are the color of emotions. They're the color of us: our feelings, energies, and in due part, who we are. Empaths have the upper hand in giving this read, as they're more able to connect with themselves and others, while emotions are simply just their ball game. However, now it's time to look past what others feel and look at what they think, with the empathic power of reading thought.

Chapter 6: Telepathy

Friday nights at the Crawford Bar were always busy. Night owls were drinking and eating, servers stumbling to get all their orders out, and smoke trailing from the kitchen created a thick layer of barbeque and burnt grease. It was between this chaos that Jeoffrey Adams sat overhearing a conversation between two men.

One of the men, a slight 30-something-year-old with an arresting stare and long hair tucked behind his ears, talked about abilities, gifts, and how he was an empath. The word empath *itself was something Jeoffrey had never heard before, but with the mention of one he did know, psychic, he stifled out a laugh, which caught the attention of the long-haired man.*

The man peeked over the shoulder of his drunken partner right at Jeoffrey. Even though the two of them were, by far, the soberest in the place, you would think that there would've been some confrontation or brawl. However, the long-haired man remained calm, and simply walked around the intoxicated man with his hand outstretched.

"The name's Bryce." After a quick introduction, Bryce took a seat next to Jeoffrey. "I'm guessing you think I'm full of it, don't you?" he said, smiling. Jeoffrey, with a rigid laugh, nodded his head.

"Guess I just don't think much of that stuff," he admitted, taking a sip of his drink. Bryce nodded, clearly understanding the hesitation as it was a view people often held for the situation. Even in such a busy place, the space between them grew silent, awkwardly so.

"I can show you that I'm not." The statement demanded Jeoffrey's attention, although he was confused. "I can show you that I'm not a fake or a looney. If nothing happens, you were right, and that's

that. However, if I do a good job, at least you'll have more faith," he suggested, a sly, yet sincere, smile on his lips. Jeoffrey had nothing better to do with his time and only a goldfish waited for him at home. In truth, he was intrigued by the stranger's offer and wanted to see how it played out. He agreed with a simple handshake and followed the man to a quieter booth in the back of the bar so Bryce could attempt to empathize with Jeoffrey.

As they sat, Bryce removed his scarf, crossed his legs, breathed rhythmically, and closed his eyes. There was a moment of silence between them, a sense of anticipation from Jeoffrey, before Bryce started laying out his synopsis:

"You're intrigued and interested in what I have to say. Although, part of you still thinks I'm only telling tales, being silly, and trying to fool you and others out of money. In your life, at this moment, you have this expansive yet unexpressed desire to have someone in your life. You have loneliness and sadness buried deep inside. You're searching for something more, a sort of emanation of the divine." Bryce shuddered before continuing. "Beneath this lies your core. There's surrendering to the divine, where you're lying beneath fields looking up at the stars. You're open to the flow of things and uncertainties, which would explain why we're here. You want love, as it's the one thing moving you through your days. That, my friend, is your true nature."

Bryce finished, opened his eyes, and was faced with Jeoffrey's stunned, speechless state of shock. He merely chugged a bit of his drink and almost coyishly said, "It was a bit rushed, of course, as I wasn't prepared. However, I think you get the gist of it. So, what do you think?"

What Is It, Anyway?

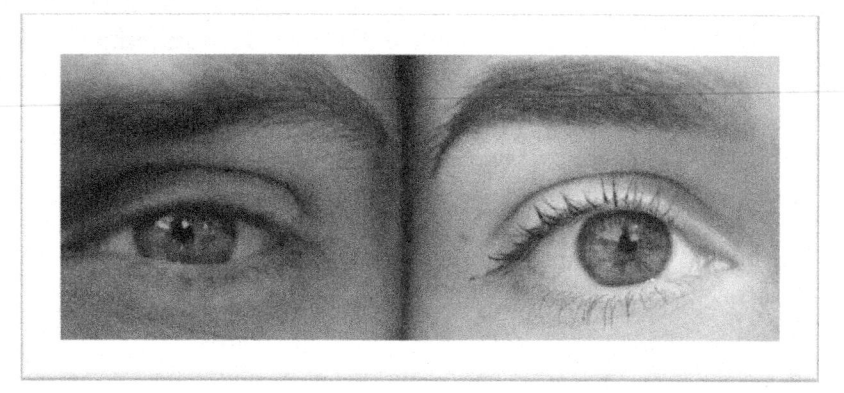

We have somewhat set ideas of what communication is and what it looks like. It's when we talk to someone or write something down; someone listens as we speak or reads the note and then responds. It's simple, and before you know it, you have a whole conversation on your hands.

Even when it's not obvious, we also use all our senses to carry us through conversations and to better understand and perceive what the other person's communicating. We scan the body language of others, listen to what they're saying, or take in other gestures such as a hug or handshake. Communication, it would seem, is simple. However, that's where you're wrong.

Telepathy, a sort of extrasensory perception (EP), defies everything we have come to know about traditional communication in that it's anything but conventional. Confusing? Perhaps it is.

Telepathy is a way of communicating without limitations of distance or the need for senses, and those with these powers use one simple device for communication: their minds. Yes, you heard me: Telepathy happens without as much as a word, hint of body language, trick, or any sense; it's simply all within the mind. In short, it's just pretty cool.

Telepathic Activities

You would think that the mention of "mind communication" would be enough—that it's all that needed to be said and that's that. However, you know me better than that by now. So, for starters, it's possible to use telepathic techniques in several ways, such as:

- Reading: Peeking inside someone else's mind by hearing or sensing their thoughts.
- Communication: Talking with the mind.
- Impression: Instilling a thought, idea, message, or image in someone else's head.
- Control: Directing or influencing another's behavior or thoughts.

A Telepathic Empath

Telepathic empaths have a better grasp on understanding those around them simply because they can pick around in the minds of others. They know what others are thinking, sense deeper emotions, and can help guide you when needed.

If you're a telepathic empath, chances are you've never had to have the uncertain, sometimes uncomfortable, conversation of "what's on your mind" simply because you already know the answer. You're always one step ahead because of your sharp senses and abilities. While you can read facial expressions, body language, and energies like they're a simple children's book about shapes. Telepathic empaths are, as a short review, simply just a unique few.

Telepathic Empath Traits

Intuition

We've covered what intuition is and how empaths use it for their own good, the good of others, and in their lives quite a bit. But it's still something worth mentioning. For telepathic empaths, intuition is the leading instrument when reading the emotions, energies, thoughts, and internal intents of those around them. They pick up all the information around them—positive, negative, and all the bits in between. That's not to say they have a higher intuition than other empaths, because there's no way of knowing that. Intuition, or strength and development of it, usually jumps and varies from person to person. However, being able to read thoughts and motivations already showcases that telepathic empaths might just have the upper hand in the intuitive department of empathic abilities.

Negativity Radars

While on the topic of intuition, telepathic empaths have another trait that takes a step away and beyond your run-of-the-mill instincts. Weighing the fact that these telepathic empaths are overly sensitive and susceptible to the energies and thoughts of those around them, they can pick up on any negative vibes and personal difficulties that others might miss. Perhaps you had a dream where a loved one was in trouble, or randomly through the day, you find yourself worrying or thinking of the well-being of others.

Fluctuating Moods

All it takes is a single thought or feeling to completely turn around and throw a telepathic empath off their game. They rarely have a stable mood simply because they're constantly being thrown by the emotions, thoughts, and workings of all the people around them. Sometimes, dealing with all of this information can become overwhelming and frustrating, so it's a good idea for telepathic empaths, and empaths in general, to get a good grip on the handle before it's too late.

Forming Bonds

Empaths, in general, have a great understanding of those around them. Telepathic ones have an even greater understanding simply because they don't even have to say a word to know the mood, motivation, thoughts, and desires of others. The relationships they form are often long-lasting, profound, and hard to break. So, usually, they've got a lot of friends and loved ones to go around. Sometimes you just have to appreciate and bathe in the benefit that is your intuition.

Space Needed

Although extraordinary intuitive abilities and great social skills and upkeep get you a long way, this can become a bit too much to handle, and for the telepathic empath, the weight can be a bit heavy. Therefore, it's not unusual for them to disappear every now and then, even when in the middle of a party. They need their alone time and place of escape to gather themselves, regain control, and work through the overload before they go on with their day.

Developing Telepathy

Meditation

I think it's become quite clear that I strongly believe in the power of meditation. It allows your mind to focus, redirect your thoughts, and keep things as apparent as it gets so that you can better connect with the consciousness of others and yourself. As you will see, the abilities are better taken care of and developed when you're at one with who you are and within your surroundings. You get that and more once you learn how to meditate, while also allowing your ability to shine through without any hiccups or mishaps.

Finding Your Strength

When you're thinking about someone, are you usually the one reaching out to them, or do you find yourself receiving a call or text from them throughout the day? Are you a receiver or a sender of messages? Finding out where your strength lies is pivotal in further developing it. Narrowing down your focus onto that single strength from the start will help you to progress faster and better. When you've got one figured out, you can move on to the other when the time is right. Once you've found your strength, it's time to fine-tune it with a bit of practice:

- Receiving messages: Perhaps you've found that you're always the one calling, texting, or reaching out with a "how are you" after someone has sent you a message. Perhaps, you just know you're on the receiving end. Either way, you need to stick to what you know best: receiving messages. The best way for you to do so would be to focus on picking up on what others are saying. It can be while you're interacting with someone, or even while you're standing in line at the grocery store. Although, that might be an invasion of privacy, to some degree. The best way to test things out (with consent) would be to grab a willing participant, ask them to send you a message, and then see whether you get anything.
- Sending messages: Sending messages can be hard at times since you don't have any foolproof way of knowing whether someone got the message or if it was a blip. However, try this: When you're greeting someone, say "hello" while thinking "goodbye." Look at their facial expression while you do this. If they seem confused, chances are they received the message you were sending. You can also try grabbing a friend, sending them a message, and seeing whether or not they get it in the end.

Practice makes perfect as they say, so simply focus on your strengths and go from there. Trust yourself and what you're experiencing, and know that you're not alone. Remember that your telepathic abilities are gifts through and through. Read my mind when I say: You've got this!

Namaste Telepathy

For your telepathic meditation today, the focus lies with clearing your mind, concentrating, and sending someone a message using only your mind, a few good breaths, and sometimes, a couple of tries too. However, before we start, it's important to mention that if you're upset with someone, it's better to leave your message unsent. Remember that, in the energy world, what you give out is what you receive, so ensure you're using your powers responsibly by only sending out positivity.

Step One:

As all our meditations up to now have started, find a quiet, comfortable, and isolated room where you can relax in a position of your choice before taking a few deep breaths. As you're breathing, allow any thoughts and feelings to come to light, observe them, and watch as they come and go.

Step Two:

As you're breathing, slowly start focusing all your attention on the vibrations and energies in your body. Feel its sting in your fingers, reach your soles, and bounce off every limb. As you acknowledge the vibration and energy of each part of your body, allow yourself to relax more and more. Once you're ready and fully relaxed, allow your focus to fall back onto your breathing.

Step Three:

As you're breathing, allow your energy to dance between your brows and on your third eye chakra. You want to activate this point and experience all it has to offer. You might experience various sensations as you go deeper into the chakra and trust that it's normal to feel these things. Don't be afraid. Simply enjoy what you're feeling, remaining relaxed and calm. Breathe and remind yourself that you're doing great, that you're in control of your thoughts, emotions, and experiences. You have the reins.

Step Four:

Once your third eye chakra is activated, start painting a picture of the person you want to send a message to. Slowly, while still imagining them, move your focus onto the person's forehead, connecting with their third eye chakra. Imagine a purple light beaming from your chakra to theirs.

Step Five:

Once you feel connected with the person, start sending them the message you want them to receive. Try to keep things short, repeating it at least five times. Allow your chakra to go into theirs, releasing all your energy.

Step Six:

Relax and bring your focus back onto yourself. Focus on your breathing and your consciousness. Remember to breathe and slowly immerse yourself back into the present as you do.

What's Next?

Following our discussion about not only reading emotions but minds too, I think it's time we jump into the next unique ability of an empath, which has something to do with visions beyond what the normal eye could see.

Chapter 7:
Clairvoyance

The sun was out, beaming onto the busy city, and kids were playing on the street while their parents grilled steaks and drank beers with their neighbors and friends. It was a pleasant day out, one of the nicest of the year. However, within one of the houses tucked away into the suburbs was a mourning family.

"Passed away peacefully in his sleep," the medics said on Monday, and today, on this warm day, was his funeral. "A loving husband, father, and grandfather," the headstone read. A no-frills yet true statement to leave him with, his children concluded. Now, his family and friends gathered in his daughter's home, picking at finger sandwiches and cups of lemonade, reminiscing on memories and qualities of a man who had a great life.

The younger children, who barely understood what was going on, played in the living room, eating plates their mothers had made them. One of which was the man's granddaughter. She was just shy of five-years-old, with thick locks of black curls and freckles from her forehead to her chin—just a few of the things she had inherited from him.

She barely gave any thought to the crowds of people giving her sympathetic looks as she colored in a dog in her coloring book. With focus, she tried to stay in the lines, a task she was horribly failing at, but still gave it her best shot. Slowly, one after the other, the mourning people made their way out of her house with an "I'm sorry" and "Let us know if you need anything," before driving off to tend to their own lives and worries.

All the while, the little girl stayed in the same spot, coloring in the dog. By now, she was the only child left on the rug, as most of her cousins and the other kids had left. The people that were left were just as old as her grandfather was. One after the other, they did the same: They met with her mother before she walked them to the door, repeated the same words as those before, and left. Her mother, she noted, looked deeply distressed and drained by the day, and wanted nothing more than to curl up in bed. Every so often, as her mother stood fanning herself with her hand, the little girl would give her an uplifting smile, ensuring her that it was okay, although unsure what the "it" was exactly. All she knew was that the smile worked.

Soon, there was only one man left. He had wrinkles and age spots all over his body, a hunched posture that never seemed to straighten, and squinted eyes over thin glasses. He's clearly older than the others, she thought as she glanced up from her drawing. It seemed as though he was in a worse shape since he was barely able to walk on his own.

Her mother had to steady him and slowly lead him out to the car that was waiting for him in the driveway. The car was just as old as him, with dents and scrapes to match his own. The girl was sure he wasn't able to drive on his own anymore. It seemed unsafe for everyone. She scrunched her eyebrows at the sight of the man slowly bending into the car. In the kitchen, she heard a door open with an aged creak. There must've been someone her mother forgot to count.

She looked up as someone slowly peeked around the sidewall of the living room. It was a man with short mopped hair that had long turned gray, with freckles dancing from his forehead to his chin. Coupled with a wide grin, he gave a playful wink, and said, "I came to say goodbye, dear." The little girl beamed at the man, nodding her head.

He sat next to her and looked at the drawing she was so invested in. Brown and yellow lines fell over the print, with lead smudges smoothed into the page from where she had used the eraser.

"It looks great! You are bound to be an artist one day," the man peeped, pulling the book up into the sun to catch a better look. She giggled, shaking her head.

"It's a bit messy. I can't seem to stay within the lines," she admitted, sighing with defeat as he gave the book back to her.

"Oh no, I think it looks just fine. After all, it's okay for things to get messy sometimes," he whispered.

They talked for a short time, and then it was time for him to leave. He simply got up and headed out the back, latching the door behind him once again. Her mother soon returned inside after finally finishing getting the other man on his way. She made her way over to the little girl and took a seat next to her on the rug.

"My dear," she started, playing with the torn cuticles of her nails. "You know that grandpa loved you so much, and that he wished he could've stayed, but that he's in a better place now, that he's resting." Her mother was barely able to blink back the tears that had formed.

The little girl, with her smile intact, simply looked up at her mother, and said, "I know mommy, grandpa was just here to say goodbye…"

Clairvoyance

The term comes from the French word *clair* (clear) and *voyance* (vision). Clairvoyance thus translates to "clear seeing" and is one of the major psychic abilities. This means gaining insight and information through extrasensory perception. It's the ability to see into the soul and intellect of all the essences within the universe, whether living or not. It's simply a synonym for being able to see clearly, often that which is unseen by others. Clairvoyants can drum into spirits, energy forms, and their own dreams, while sometimes being able to interpret the messages they've received. If you are clairvoyant, you're able to receive intuitive information in a variety of ways, such as colors, movements, and symbols that often happen in the mind's eye. Pretty cool, right?

The problem is that those with this ability often walk around not knowing of their psychic power, simply because it's often very subtle, viewed as imagination, or brushed off as nothing more than a quick play on lights, eyesight, or other factors. However, the truth is much denser than that. Clairvoyants are powerful beings, whether they can see it now or not.

Traits of Clairvoyants

The Sight

Clairvoyants' sights are often flooded with flashes of lights and colors, almost as if the world around them is tearing open. Although it might seem strange or startling, these glittering lights and colored dots are often spirits looking to send you information and messages. The same goes for those moments where you could've sworn you saw something move in the corner of your eye. It might merely be spirits floating around, and you happen to catch one of them while they were on their way. Another way in which you can see colors is that which envelops people. If you've read Chapter 5, you know that I'm hinting at auras. Reading auras and seeing them clearly is a department you particularly thrive in. Besides, seeing things clearly is what you're good at!

Dreams

Clairvoyants are the dreamers of the empathic world, and they tend to dream whenever they're asleep or awake—either way works fine. When they're awake, their minds often wander, zone out frequently, and imagine things to the point where they would much rather prefer living there instead. Clairvoyance has to do with seeing and visualization, after all, so who can blame them, really? It's a significant part of who they are, and it comes naturally. When they go to bed, however, that's when the dreaming starts. Clairvoyants have sights that work on overdrive at all times, even when they're fast asleep. Their dreams are often vivid, exploding with bright lights, colors, and imagery that makes it hard for them to distinguish between what's real and what's fantasy.

Different Outlooks

Clairvoyants have sights like no other—it's what guides them through their lives and makes them unique. Their stances in life allows them to see, appreciate, and connect with the finer things in life, the beautiful and creative things to give your sight that additional touch of polish. Clairvoyants have strong visualization skills that make them the person you call when you have a problem. It would almost seem like they've got it all figured out. They see direction in life, map out plans in their heads, and see the wires and knots that connect all the things in life. So, yes, to some degree, they've unriddled most of life. Don't get me wrong, they've still got challenges of their own.

Seeing Better

Clairvoyant empaths are deeply intuitive, and when they train their intuition, it can be well used to strengthen their own energy and abilities to better understand and make sense of all the images they receive. So, the key to upping your intuition is to meditate, understand subtle energy, and learn to read chakras, or simply developing your intuitive abilities as discussed before.

Additionally, you should learn to take on and accept your awareness of the world around you and what you're seeing. Remember that if you're clairvoyant, your world is made up of images of all sorts—embrace them. Look out for those images that pop into your head, those glimpses you catch from time to time, and listen to your dreams, and those strange things you might see; they might just be messages waiting for you to receive. It might be hard to accept that you see things differently than most people around you, but it's essential to do so and trust in your abilities and sight. Once you accept who you are and trust your eyes (both those on the outside and inside), you'll be able to make sense of the world and use your gifts for the greater good.

Strengthening your abilities and learning to trust and work with your abilities is a great step toward living your life with enhanced sight. Start off by exercising your third eye, using your powers deliberately, being creative, and accepting all that you see. You're unique, and once you accept all that you are, you'll be able to see what a beautiful world you've been gifted.

Visualization Meditation

Since clairvoyance is all about seeing clearly, I thought we should explore a meditation focused on visualization. The purpose is to deepen your meditation and direct your mind toward specific results and images by using your inner sight and imagination. Therefore, although there will be a lot of "see this" and "see that" guidelines, the ultimate key lies in the details and visualizations you create.

Step One:

Take a seat somewhere you can be alone for a few minutes, ensuring that there's nothing that can disturb your visualization or relaxation. Ensure your space is comfortable, safe, and soothing. Take a seat or lie down, whichever one you prefer. For now, simply take a few deep breaths, allowing your body to relax. Close your eyes as you inhale, and roll out the tension from your limbs as you exhale. Push away any thoughts, feelings, or images that come along, as you don't need them at this moment. Relax and center yourself in this time and space of nothingness. Breathe and relax.

Step Two:

When you're ready, move your consciousness to a space far away from here: a field of untouched grass and blooming flowers. Simply focus on the blades of grass below your feet. What do you see? Focus on the color and texture, the small ants scurrying among the blades, and the soft movements caused by the wind. Focus on a beetle that has landed at your feet, studying its body, legs, and wings. Follow it as it flies up to reveal a large mass of water in front of you.

Step Three:

Step closer to see the water as it gently flows and crashes. See the inhabitants: the fish, frogs, and insects. Study each one with care and curiosity. See the sun reflect its color onto the stream, blending in with the clear brown bottom. See the water ripple as a deer makes its way to drink, and follow your gaze from its reflection to its body. Study the way he gracefully moves to drink. As he bends his neck, see his tail whisp away flies, and study the way his antlers curve and bend. Pay attention to each individual hair and spot on his frame. What do you see?

Step Four:

As you gently stretch your view, see the grass and flowers behind the deer, the way they break under his feet, and refold around him. Study the dirt and rocks as they fall into the water as he continues his drink.

Follow the forest as it crawls up the mountain ridge. See the mountain ripple and grow toward its peak, almost scraping the clouds. Note the rays and color of the sun as it slowly tucks itself away behind the triangular shape. Feel the warmth and enlightenment of nature and the energy around you.

Step Five:

If you wish to go past the mountain, or up to the clouds, do so with pleasure. See and evaluate every part of the earth and the images and messages it brings to you. Note how you're feeling in this space, the sensations you feel, the vibrations against your skin, and the soft dance of colors and lights around you. Feel and see the space as clearly and vividly as you can. Allow yourself to breathe and explore.

Step Six:

Whenever you're ready, take a few deep breaths and remind yourself that you're sitting or lying down comfortably. Remind yourself about the room you're in and that you're safe. Slowly bring your presence back to the room and reality of your life, remembering all that you were able to see and receive.

What's Next?

So far, we've discussed what it takes to see as a clairvoyant empath would, how you can set your sight on your abilities and work through what you have to, and all the abilities of other types of empaths and how you can develop them. Now it's time we proceed to the next step: learning how to take care of yourself with some self-care and protection.

Part III:
An Empath's Guide to Self-Care

Chapter 8:
Unblocking and Balancing Chakras

"Your honor, according to Mr. Charles's statement, Miss Adams is anything but fit to take care of their daughter. She's on non-prescription drugs, drinks excessively, and is in counseling for severe psychological problems. My client says the house is bare of furniture too. She's barely scraping by while taking care of an additional three children from her previous relationships. My client fears for his daughter's safety and believes she would be safer under his sole care. Mr. Charles asks that you not only consider her bad habits but also her character," the attorney finished, taking a seat next to the father.

On the other side of the courtroom sat Jane Adams, the mother, with a vile aftertaste in her mouth as she listened to the assassination attempt her ex-husband had planned out. The claims he made were false, exaggerated, and laughable. Yes, Jane enjoyed a glass of wine with her dinner every now and then, but she never had more than one. There were no pills or powders; there never were. She did go to therapy after her daughter's birth, but had left it years ago. The most outlandish claim by far was that of her will to provide for her kids. She would do anything to ensure that they had full bellies, healthy meals, an education, and a warm bed. She always gave them the very best she could.

It was all lies he had twisted together, and both of them knew it. Jane tried speaking up to protest against the outrageous assertions; however, her lawyer was quick to stop her.

"Talk only when the judge asks you to; nothing more, nothing less," he said.

For a moment, in her eyes at least, his professionalism was slung with cowardice. She knew her lawyer wasn't to blame for her ex-husband's claims and her faltering image. Yet still, she wanted to blame someone, anyone. Right now, she held him responsible. It was even more disheartening when Judge Turkins, an elderly woman with her glasses pushed to the rim of her nose, didn't ask Jane for her side of the story. She simply cleared her throat, gave Jane a superficial look, and said, "The custody will remain shared at 50/50. Next case..."

It seemed that the evidence was in her favor and that his lies were, at least, clear. Yet still, there was an itch in her throat that she couldn't explain. Jane pushed her chair away from the table, stood up, and without as much as a word or second look, stormed out of the court to her car and drove off.

She was happy about the verdict given by the judge. She was afraid of losing her daughter, and as soon as she heard the junk flowing from her former spouse, she thought he had a sure win under his belt. Luckily, that wasn't the case today. So, why did she feel so violated, shamed, traumatized, and unjustified? She didn't speak her truth, defend herself, and have her say. It ate away at her. Did her side of the story, her reputation, her voice, mean nothing?

Right before her turn onto Maple Street, she pulled off to the side of the road and rested her car on the dirt shoulder. As she sat in silence, tears streamed down her cheeks. She hadn't dared cry in court. She took the shame as it came her way and without a peep. Her throat tightened as if it were closing in on itself with a burning scrape as she allowed herself to feel the disappointment and frustration of the day.

She wanted a chance to clear her name, tell her truth, and prove that she was a good mother. She just didn't want to be silenced the way she was. She didn't say anything, not that she was allowed to. He got away with it, regardless. It was an attack on her throat chakra, her vishuddha, an attack on her character, her energy, her child, and her family. She felt helpless as all she could do was sit in her car, feel what she had to feel, and cry.

Chakras

Throughout this book, I have mentioned energies, third eyes, and chakras here and there, and much to your demise, have not discussed or explained them one bit. Don't worry, I noticed, and you can rest assured that it was intentional as all you need to know will be discussed right here. See, I won't leave you hanging.

What Are They?

In the sacred language of Hinduism, Sanskrit, "Chakra" or to be more precise, "cakra," means wheel. I know, not as climactic but all will make sense in a moment. We all know what wheels are and what they do: they're circular spinning tools that help us get where we want to go. As a spiritual concept, chakras work much like your tires. They're spinning disks, representing the central points or channels through which our energy travels, which in turn, gets us where we want to go in our lives.

So, why is it that everyone keeps going on about them? If they're always spinning inside our bodies, won't they just do that: spin? Not quite. Just like how you have to take your car in for maintenance and check to see whether your tire has a puncture, you need to keep an eye on your chakras. They have to be opened and aligned to do their job and not "deflate" on us.

Sadly, very few of us get taught how to manage chakras since it's not as widely discussed as going for a jog or eating some fruit. Keeping your chakras open and aligned is just as important for your entire body: nerves, organs, brain, body, and all. Chakras supply your entire body with the energy it needs, and without that subtle pump of vibrations, your body won't be able to work at its best. So, that's what chakras are, why we need to know more, and why we need to open them up and keep them in mind.

Meeting Your Chakras

So, now you know what chakras are, why you need to take care of them, and all the basics. However, if we don't dive deeper into the specifics, you won't get too far. Hence, it's time to open up our portals and position ourselves to look at where they're located and all the types there are.

Before we jump into it, it's important to note that the number of chakras we have is unknown, with some claiming that we have up to 114. That's quite the quantity, right? However, before you start to sweat, I won't be going through them all. This isn't the *Venmurasu* (the world's lengthiest book) of empath self-helps. Instead, we'll be sticking to the main guys, which are only seven—phew. In summary, these primary chakras run along your spine, starting at the base and going up to the crown of your head. It's almost like a Christmas tree with lights... but I think the image below showcases it best.

Root Chakra (Muladhara)

Your root chakra is located at the base of your spine and is the spiritual backing of your whole body, like how a tree's roots are what keep it living and grounded to the earth. This chakra is your primary source of energy that's responsible for your sense of security, survival, stability, grounding, and more. It affects how we connect to the world, and when it's imbalanced, everything else will be thrown off. Here's all the characteristics and methods of engagements you need to know about your muladhara chakra:

- Color: red
- Element: earth
- Sense: smell
- Crystals: Red Jasper, Hematite, Onyx
- Herbs: ashwagandha, dandelion root, ginger
- Yoga poses: wide-leg forward fold, Malasana squats, mountain, warrior I, tree
- Affirmation: I am...

Sacral Chakra (Svadhishthana)

Your sacral chakra sits below your belly button and above your pubic bone. This spinning disk is associated with your emotions, creativity, self-worth, intuition, compassion, adaptability, pleasures, and desires. With this chakra standing as it should, you will feel more than great; however, when it's off, you're more likely to experience emotional outbursts, creativity blocks, and desire-obsessed thoughts, which could throw off the energy and rhythm of your overall life. Here's all the characteristics and methods of engagements you need to know about your svadhisthana chakra:

- Color: orange
- Element: water
- Sense: taste
- Crystals: Tiger's Eye, Carnelian, Sunstone
- Herbs: damiana, ylang ylang, rose
- Yoga Poses: pigeon, goddess, warrior II, bridge, lizard
- Affirmation: I feel...

Solar Plexus Chakra (Manipura)

Your solar plexus chakra is located in the upper part of your stomach, in the center of your body. Just like its position, the chakra is in charge of the center of your self and identity. It's associated with everything that has to do with you: your ego, self-esteem, confidence, self-empowerment, and every thought or feeling you have about yourself. When imbalanced, that little voice inside that tells you you're great might not be as bright as you would like it to be. Here's all the characteristics and methods of engagements you need to know about your manipura chakra:

- Color: yellow
- Element: fire
- Sense: sight
- Crystals: Citrine, Pyrite, Amber
- Herbs: lemongrass, milk thistle, chamomile

- Yoga Poses: boat, twists, warrior III, triangle
- Affirmation: I can...

Heart Chakra (Anahata)

Your heart chakra is right in the center of your chest, just above your heart, hence the name. As you could've guessed, it's responsible for all things associated with love: adoration for self and others, compassion, trust, attachment, and passion. When your heart chakra is a bit broken off, your oh-so-loving nature will be in reverse and quite downbeat, to say the least. Here's all the characteristics and methods of engagements you need to know about your anahata chakra:

- Color: green
- Element: air
- Sense: touch
- Crystals: Rose Quartz, Jade, Malachite
- Herbs: hawthorn berry, rose, jasmine
- Yoga Poses: reverse plank, upward-facing dog, camel, wheel, humble warrior
- Affirmation: I love...

Throat Chakra (Vishuddha)

Your throat chakra, as the name implies, is in your throat. I don't know about you, but for me, that screams speech. You would be right to assume so, as this chakra is all about self-expression, communication, confidence to express inner truth, being heard by others, and more. When your throat chakra is silenced, you're holding in your true feelings, keeping back your voice, and you might find yourself, for example, feeling weak and quietened. Here's all the characteristics and methods of engagements you need to know about your vishuddha chakra:

- Color: blue
- Element: ether

- Sense: sound
- Crystals: Lapis Lazuli, Aquamarine, Kyanite
- Herbs: slippery elm, clary sage, chamomile
- Yoga Poses: fish, plow, shoulder stand
- Affirmation: I speak...

Third Eye Chakra (Ajna)

Your third eye is set between your eyebrows and can be seen as a way of connecting you with the outside world and beyond. It's believed that this chakra controls your intuition, intellect, wisdom, inspiration, and spiritual power. When your third eye is balanced, you're said to be free from earthly attachments and attuned with what's around you. While if not, you feel clouded and almost stuck without a way of moving forward. Here's all the characteristics and methods of engagements you need to know about your ajna chakra:

- Color: indigo
- Element: light
- Sense: intuition
- Crystals: Amethyst, Purple fluorite, Labradorite
- Herbs: passionflower, sandalwood, sage
- Yoga Poses: child, dolphin, folded eagle, forward fold
- Affirmation: I see...

Crown Chakra (Sahastrara)

Your crown chakra sits at the very top of your head, like a crown. The chakra is the highest of them all, which makes sense, considering that this chakra connects you to a higher consciousness and spirituality. It also ties you toward your inner self, others, the cosmos, the universe, and the divine. When your crown is tilted, you're more likely to disconnect from the world and tangle the lines of pure consciousness. Here's all the characteristics and methods of engagements you need to know about your sahastrara chakra:

- Color: violet

- Element: thought
- Senses: all senses
- Crystals: Selenite, Clear Quartz, Lepidolite
- Herbs: lavender, gotu kola, tulsi leaf
- Yoga Poses: headstand, tree, Savasana, corpse
- Affirmation: I know...

When Chakras Get Clogged

When it comes to understanding your chakras, there's a bit more to it than simply knowing the definition and primary types. You have to know, understand, and be able to identify times when some of your chakras might be blocked or imbalanced (not too little or too much), as it can affect your life and energy greatly, which in turn, can throw the entire ball off its route and make everything fall apart. That's not something you want. Keeping your chakras in shape will ensure that you live a fulfilled and balanced life. So, what are the warning signs?

Blockages and imbalances can show themselves in various physical or non-physical ways. It might feel like something isn't quite right, you start to lose focus, get sick, and then you get sick again, or it simply feels like everything's falling short. It could depend on the severity of the block or imbalance or which chakra is in pain. It all depends, I'm afraid. But, we'll get to all that in a minute.

I want to stress the importance of having balanced and unclogged chakras. In all simplicity, it's the way things have to be! When chakras are as they should be, so will you and your empathic abilities. You allow yourself to see your inner self in its best light and potential. Remember that there is a world of wisdom and strength within you. All you need is to take a moment to look inside to feel and acknowledge all you are. Only then will you understand how deeply it runs within your veins and how truly remarkable you are! The best way to do this is by opening and aligning our chakras, looking after our energies, developing our abilities, and taking on the best versions of ourselves. All while being balanced, centered, and at peace.

Recognize

Now that you know why it's important to have your chakras just right, you need the tools and guides on how to recognize a chakra that is slightly tilting on the one side.

Root Chakra

Suppose you've found yourself feeling frustrated, pessimistic, unstable, or ungrounded in your life, perhaps with a touch or two of back pain, abdominal discomfort, or needing more oomph to get out of bed. Perhaps, you feel disconnected from yourself and the world around you, or there's a kick of digestive irritability. You might have too much energy and feel greedy or excessive in your behaviors. Whatever the case, some emotional downfalls and physical declines can signal that your root chakra has been pulled out and unearthed. Although there are plenty of other signs and tells you should take a look at, it might be time to rebalance and unclog your chakra for good, right from the root.

Sacral Chakra

You might display various physical ailments and shortcomings, such as pain in the lower body, hormonal instability, infertility, and uterine concerns. You may also lack creativity, inspiration, and sympathy. You might also be bombarded with obsessive thoughts, energetic lethargy, and emotional flux. Once again, be sure to dive deeper into the signs further. However, those mentioned can give you a good idea of whether or not your sacral chakra might need some tuning.

Solar Plexus Chakra

With your solar plexus chakra, you've got a few annoying things to bear, such as ulcers, indigestion, and some stomach pangs. There are also a few severe conditions, such as diabetes and liver problems. Your mood might be on edge, depressed, all over the place, and in doubt. Perhaps, you notice hints of narcissism, resentment, or cynicism. Look into your symptoms further, but you might be on the wrong side of the road and will have to take a turn or two to get back on track.

Heart Chakra

When your heart chakra is off, you could fall into cardiovascular and respiratory diseases and pains in your upper back, chest, and shoulders. Instead of love, you could showcase aggression, cynicism, jealousy, self-sabotage, self-victimization, and resentment or hatred toward yourself and others. All of these will need some further backing, but overall, I would say that you need to get your chakra back onto the positive because love is simply much better than all that.

Throat Chakra

Your throat chakra will, as you could've guessed, affect your voice, ears, throat, and mouth. You might experience a tense jaw and pained shoulder. You might also have headaches, migraines, and frequent colds. There are two ways this can affect you socially. One way could lead you to a place where you're dominating conversations, gossiping, lying compulsively, and stepping on the toes of others. The second way could lead you to retract and isolate yourself from others completely, such as showcasing timidity, poor boundaries, and excessive inhibition up to social anxiety. It's no fun, as you can imagine, and the time to take back your voice is now.

Third Eye Chakra

With imbalances or blockages in your third eye, you might commonly experience problems with your brain, sight, and hearing, such as migraines, blurry vision, and common brain fog. You might also have trouble tapping into your intuition, dealing with your imagination, learning and retaining information, mental health, and working your way to understanding and trusting others. Without you truly opening your third eye, you won't be able to see and know what you have to. And you simply can't walk through life blind.

Crown Chakra

With your crown leaning to the side, you might deal with constant migraines and headaches, poor coordination, and problems remembering what you should. Furthermore, you might alienate, dissociate, or disconnect yourself from the outside world and lose your purpose. Perhaps you block those around you, narrow your mind, and numb yourself to their feelings, thoughts, and beliefs. If you can't accept and look after your crown chakra, you won't catch it before it falls.

Purify

Before we get down to how you can purify your blocked and unbalanced chakras, I wanted to explain how you should use the following information. Remember when you were getting to know your chakras and I listed all those colors, herbs, and such? I want you to keep them in mind while reading how you can set your chakras straight, and work on individual ones by using their bullet points where appropriate. I'll be using one or two as examples, but the information below applies to them all (they are connected as a system, after all). All you have to do is make a replacement here and there to focus on one at a time.

Using Elements

Spend time connecting with your element by doing activities that bring you closer to it, such as zen-ing out on a walk and spending time in nature to cleanse, balance, and ground your root chakra, or bathing in the sunlight to work on your third eye.

Nutrition

The key to chakra nutrition is sticking to your colors while keeping a stern eye on nutritional values and wholesomeness. For example, eat yellow foods that are easy to digest, like bananas, corn, and pineapples, to feed your solar plexus chakra. Similarly, eat your greens, reds, indigos, oranges, and blues when needed, while feeding your spirit when it comes to your crown. Most importantly, ensure that every meal counts and that you sip on your teas and waters, while also stocking up on your herbs (as long as they're edible).

Get Physical

Your chakras are connected to different body parts. Therefore, focusing on these body parts will do you wonders. You can do some stretching, yoga, and other general exercises. You can try stretching and moving your hips to open your sacral chakra and strengthen your core to connect with your third chakra. So, give those yoga poses a try and do some more research on ways to cleanse your chakras while breaking a sweat and moving around.

Blend With Colors

The colors associated with the chakras are keys to opening, balancing, and cleansing your chakras. Therefore, when any of your chakras feels a bit off, simply surround yourself with the tints and shades associated with it however you can. Wear clothes, jewelry, and accessories of the same hue. Any other things that share the same pigment will do. Why not pick up a bouquet of indigo flowers on your way home to help along your sixth chakra?

Connect and Appreciate

Oftentimes, the best way to truly heal and cleanse your chakras is by taking time to connect with yourself and finding ways to express your love and care toward others. You can try some grounding techniques, meditations, therapy sessions, journaling, self-care routines, and volunteering. You can use each chakra's affirmation introduction to create something personal and of your own, coupled with their own mantras (which you'll have to look up). Furthermore, try and enjoy the finer things in life and embrace your originality. Remember to sing and dance when you get the chance, listen to music, or sit outside, spend time with your crystal, and do the things you love most with the people you care about or alone.

Chakra Contemplation

When it comes to cleaning your chakras, there's no better way than getting up close and personal by not only seeing them inside of your body, but feeling and connecting with every pulse they vibrate.

Step One:

Take your place in a quiet, relaxing space. Sit comfortably with your hands on your knees, palms facing up, and gently close your eyes.

Step Two:

Inhale deeply, allowing your belly to expand and shoulders to rise for a count of four, and hold it there for an additional four. Count in your head if it helps. Then, gently exhale through your mouth, allowing your stomach to contract and shoulders to fall for a count of four, and hold the empty breath for another four. You can now start breathing normally.

Step Three:

Look inside your body and picture your root chakra, a red vibrating lotus pulsing with energy. Allow it to gain energy with each breath you take. See it as it spins faster and faster with the growth. Sit with your root chakra for a moment, allowing it to gain ferocity and strength. Then move onto your next chakra and then the next. See the color shine within each one, the way they spin and vibrate as they gain power and velocity, and allow yourself to sit, for a moment, admiring each one. Slowly work your way up to your crown chakra, taking your time to do so.

Step Four:

Once you've run through all your chakras, allow the system to vibrate and color your insides with energy. Feel the warm and static pulses it sends through your entire body. Return to a deep inhale and to your breathing from Step Two.

What's Next?

After learning how to manage your chakras, you can now focus on another essential element of taking care of yourself as an empath: cleansing your energy, staying in touch with your chakras, and striving toward a better, cleaner self.

Chapter 9:
Cleansing and Healing Your Energy

To say that Brenda Stone was nervous would be an understatement. She was losing it, as some would say, but in a more relaxed and composed way, if there was such a thing. She never was much of an anxious person, always steady, calm, and in control of how she felt. But not today. Today she was on her toes and nervous about every tick and sting around her.

No one likes to feel worried or stressed, but Brenda especially loathed the feeling; she hated pacing back and forth, for no apparent reason, for minutes on end. She supposed it was a way to keep herself busy, gather her thoughts, and somehow tire out the unsettling feeling tugging at her core. Brenda wasn't an anxious person, never had been, but today all it took was a single trip and she was pacing her living room.

You see, it had only been about three weeks since the lockdown started, and Brenda preferred ordering in. Sometimes her husband agreed to make an errand or two. She wasn't ashamed to admit that he had more guts than her, so he made the trips and returned to a skeptical, overprotective wife. As soon as he stepped into the front door, she would strip him down, slather his body in sanitizer, and throw his clothes straight into the bin, with a new outfit already waiting for him.

She knew that she was being a bit dramatic and that her precautions might be seen as over-the-top and frantic, but she didn't care. She played it safe and avoided running into any chances or risks. It was this whole disease thing: It made her feel off, on edge, and always planning for that one more step ahead. However, it also kept her indoors and away from the world outside. Today, her husband was feeling a bit under the weather, so she had to go to the supermarket on her own.

"Medication, snacks, toilet paper, milk," her grocery list read. It was short and sweet—nothing she couldn't handle! For the most part, she was taking the whole outside-in-pandemic thing rather well. The ride to the local shop was easy, almost desolate, and smooth sailing. Her nerves were steel, and she even sang along to a song on the radio. All was good, and nothing was wrong.

The problem came when she turned into the lot and searched for a place to park. A few cars were parked here and there, a surprising amount considering their situation. That's when her nerves started to spike up. For some reason, finding a spot seemed to be an impossible task, and left her questioning every spot she saw. Don't ask her why, as she didn't know herself, but she did. It took her a good 45 minutes before she finally settled for a spot in the back, surrounded by very few vehicles, and if she had to make it back fast, she could.

After one problem was solved, however, another one stepped up: What if the store is out of toilet paper? she contemplated. She wasn't ready to drive to another store and do the whole parking thing again. Once was plenty, after all. She thought about how many people were in the supermarket, counting car doors to get the maximum estimate. She wondered what her chances were of catching the disease and bringing it home to her already ill husband. She looked around her entire car for another mask, scarf, or hat, anything that could double-up on her already excessive layers of protection. She was nervous and scared. She hadn't been out for weeks. It took her an additional 30 minutes to get in and out of the store, and she only returned home with the medication her husband needed.

"Fast in, fast out," she told him.

The whole trip had thrown her energy off, and now she was pacing around, in hopes of setting things right. It didn't work. Her mind was fogged, and it seemed like nothing could help her now.

"Honey?" her husband said as he peeked around the corner, giving a slight cough as he smiled. "Come here." He ushered her into their bedroom. Sitting neatly at the side of the bed was a foot bath, plugged in and bubbling; her essential oils and salts were neatly set out on the bedside table.

"Calm down, won't you?" He winked, rolling himself back into bed. Smiling, Brenda sat with her feet in the water, splashing in lavender and rose oils, and a touch of salt, into the water, before closing her eyes.

What was I thinking? she thought. That'll teach me to overload on negativity and news. It will take a while, but we'll be fine. Get yourself together, Brenda! With that, all her stress and worries were gone.

Why Clean Inside

We all know to brush our teeth, wash our bodies, brush our hair, and throw on some clean drawers and clothes. However, very few of us take the time to clean our energy. It's just as important as giving yourself a good scrub down, especially when you're an empath. Empaths pick up a lot of emotions, feelings, and metaphorical dirt and filth along their usual routes, and they might need a few run-downs with the exfoliating glove before all of it can come off. You must be wondering, who cleanses their energy? Why wasn't I taught this as a child? I honestly don't know, but a good guess would be that no one really considers it or remembers to do so. Nonetheless, cleaning your aura, energy, and overall spirit is a sure must if you want to get and stay healthy, aligned with your true self, and feel like your best self every day. So, always remember to wash up and stay clean!

Tools and Toiletries

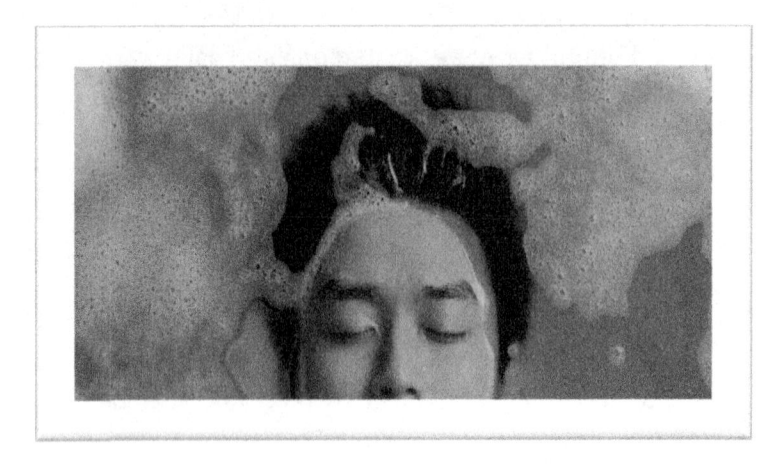

I don't know about you, but I have my bathroom preferences. Maybe you prefer a loofah or exfoliating glove over a washcloth, or a body wash over a bar of soap. We have our preferences, tools, and ways of doing things when we're cleaning up and taking on the day. As I've stated before, caring for and cleaning up your energy is no different than taking a bath: You still need all the tools, products, and help you can get. So, here are a few things you can give a try.

Using Salt

Salt is a fantastic cleanser for your body, mind, and soul. In fact, simply keeping a bowl around the home can do wonders for you! I know, who knew? Well, quite a few people, actually. For centuries, salt (especially Himalayan salt) has been used to protect, purify, and cleanse homes and individuals while also dispelling negativity and releasing attachments that aren't that healthy to hold. However, if you're looking for more intimate and precise usages, I've got you covered:

- Cleansing and protecting salt scrub: Scrubs are meant to cleanse and exfoliate the body; they remove impurities, slough dead skin, and leave behind a finer, more even and glowing skin and complexion. Just as we use scrubs for the outside, this salt scrub helps you get that lighter feel from the inside out. The assortment of Epsom salt, sea salt, rosemary sprigs, jojoba oil, sage, vetiver, and lavender essential oils cleanses your energy and protects you from negativity, while also leaving you refreshed and rejuvenated every time.

- Himalayan bath salt: After you've filled the tub with some warm water, try throwing in some Himalayan salt, and ylang-ylang essential oils with some vanilla. This combination of bathtub add-ons is the ultimate way of cleansing your energy, kicking away negativity, and soaking the stress of any day right off.
- Detox soaking salt: Our bodies, minds, and souls go through a lot during the day, and we put them through quite a bit. Therefore, needing a detox every now and then shouldn't be a surprise. A soaking salt made from sea salt, blue clay, and eucalyptus oil is the perfect mix to clear your energy and throw off any negativity. Detoxing is a must and this combination has just enough of all the right stuff to scrub your physical and spiritual self until they're almost new.
- Salt and showers: I know that most of what I've said was more focused on having a tub. I know not everyone has a shower and bath, all-in-one, or a bath at all. Therefore, I should mention that all of these methods and tools can still be used if you only have a shower. Simply fill a bowl with some water and throw all your salts and oils in there, allowing it to marinate, before splashing it over yourself, or just mixing some salt in with your foams or shampoos.
- Salty surroundings: Another way to help cleanse your own energy and that of your surroundings, is to throw some salt in little bowls and stack them around the corners and on the tables where you can, and allow them to rest overnight before you clean them up. You could also stick a slab of salt on your desk or somewhere close.

Stripping Sage

It's believed that burning sage promotes health, wisdom, and positivity, and has been used in cultures all over for centuries. Smoke cleansing is a renowned practice that even science can't deny. Apart from its energy-cleansing abilities, it purifies the air, kills bacteria, and boosts the overall well-being of the burner. Smoke is, simply said, the way to go. So, I think all that's left is to grab all the things you need and light a match:

- White sage, lavender, and eucalyptus: This combination is a fantastic herbal remedy known for its healing and cleansing properties, while also renewing your tired mind and allowing room for Zen. You could add some eucalyptus to offer some additional cleansing and grounding. White sage on its own is excellent for a classic smoke cleanse of your crystals and space, or a quick touch up on your aura.

Any other aromatics, such as rose or thyme, will get the job done too, as they offer that added benefit or two, because let's be honest, the scent of sage might not be for everyone. Burning away your worries, negative thoughts, and energies is a superb way of conforming your mind and enhancing your intuitive and empathic abilities. Also, you'll just feel like you're on top of the world afterward, and who doesn't want that?

Healing Crystals

Crystals have the unique ability to help ground, center, and raise our vibrations so that we're more at peace with ourselves. They're excellent energy protectors that deflect negative energies and absorb them into themselves. Crystals help calm and soothe the empathetic soul while allowing you to tune into yourself, recharge your battery, and take a break.

Some crystals are especially beneficial for empaths because they're good at absorbing and deflecting negative energy, helping you work through your emotions and thoughts, and giving you a shield of protection and health like no other. However, I won't lie, I found it especially hard to pull together a list, since crystals are just too great, and the varieties are not only endless but fantastic. So, I've simply decided to list for you all the stones that fit right in with the empathic needs and personality, hoping that you will give them all a good search when you're done here:

- Clear Quartz
- Selenite
- Black Tourmaline
- Fluorite
- Labradorite
- Black Obsidian
- Rose Quartz
- Hematite
- Angelite
- Red Jasper
- Lapis Lazuli
- Amethyst
- Aventurine
- Aquamarine
- Smoky Quartz
- Green Jade
- Moonstone
- Sodalite
- Fire Agate
- Black Kyanite
- Rutilated Quartz
- Petalite
- Lepidolite
- Sugilite
- Charoite
- Blue Apatite
- Malachite
- Citrine
- Agate

- Jet
- Bloodstone
- Angel Aura Quartz
- Magnetite
- Purple Jade
- Healer's Gold
- Lodestone
- Shungite
- Tiger's Eye
- Turquoise

How to Pick and Use Crystals

When picking the right crystal for you, you should look at what's missing in your life and what you need. From there, let your gut guide your decision. You might find yourself drawn to one in particular, or you just know which one you have to go for. Your subconscious tends to know which crystal you need, and if not, simply do some research and spend time thinking about which one would fit you the best.

I won't be going into the broader idea of using crystals, but instead, I'll give you a few main points on using crystals as an empath to make the most of your energies and powers:

- Always have at least one protection stone on you at all times. Try using them as jewelry, where it touches your skin and is the most beneficial.
- Keep the vibes around you clean and chipper. Surround yourself with as many beneficial stones as you can, such as those that uplift your energy, protect you and your home, and so on. The more stones and minerals, the better.
- Strengthen your emotional well-being by meditating with your crystal in hand, and using it during any spiritual activities and empathic ability development exercises.
- Look after your stone and remember to cleanse them regularly by holding it under cold, running water,

immersing it in sea salt, placing it in sun or moonlight, or smudging your crystal with sage or other herbs.

A Place in Nature

Nature is the natural home of an empath's vibrancy. Sometimes, all it takes for you to clean your energy and ground yourself is simply walking with the grass between your toes or sitting under the shade of a tree.

Nature is a powerful source that presents you with a calming space and a great selection of elements that can feed and heal you at all times, while also allowing you to rest. One such element is water.

When you're eating a meal and you spill some on yourself, you get up and wipe it off with some water, right? We do this because we know that water cleans things. Just as it can clean off a stain, water can clean us from the inside out. Water is, after all, an element that can help you connect to your energy and help you heal. Therefore, the key is to be one with moisture. However, be sure to charge your water with intentions and affirmations. Say things like, "May this water cleanse my energy," "May I feel revived and clear," or "As I drink the water, may it help me heal, feed my energy, and cleanse me from the inside and out, body and soul."

Essential Oils

If you've ever used essential oils, you know what a great energy boost and reviver it can be, and also why so many people love it and use it so dearly. Simply add a drop of your favorite oil to a diffuser, bath, or onto your pillow, wrists, neck, and bottom of your feet. I personally recommend trying out some rosemary oil, spruce oil, grapefruit oil, or tangerine oil to assist you in cleansing and releasing your energy. Aromatherapy meets relaxation, and more. It's simply an empath's dream.

The Sound of Music

Sounds are simply vibrations. That's why clapping, singing, humming, or playing an instrument works wonders when cleansing and dispersing energies and elevating the vibrations around you. Why don't you give sound bowls, tuning forks, or other forms of restorative music a try? Personally, I'm more of a sound bowl type of person, as it's tuned to fit and work on each chakra. On the other hand, perhaps all you need is to turn down the noise and spend some quiet time with yourself.

Soothing Sprays

You could try combining all you've learned by setting up salt sprays, essential oil sprays, or crystal sprays to cleanse your aura and space. The best part of it all is that you can even create some yourself. Here are some ideas:

- Aura mist: This is a spray infused with black tourmaline and rose quartz to remove unwanted energies and shift your vibration.
- Energy cleaning mist: This is a palo santo essential oil that works as a powerful energy cleanser and positivity magnet.
- Water elemental spray: This is a citrus, lavender, and eucalyptus essential oil, with essences of amazonite and aquamarine crystals to really clarify you whenever and wherever you are.

Taking Breaths

I won't go on about meditation, because I've discussed it quite a lot and there are still plenty of scripts to come. However, just take note that meditation is a great way of getting everything sorted and tidy, so it's best to get in as much of it as you can.

Now, you should also note that meditation is intentional. Well, duh, right? The point I'm trying to make is that when you intentionally try to push out the negativity and straining emotions from your body, everything else simply starts to fall into place. Therefore, any sort of technique that works for you will get the job done, whether it be breathwork, or any other method, such as those above. Here are some techniques to try:

- Try the emotional freedom technique (EFT). You know how acupuncture involves sticking a lot of needles into your pressure points to relieve pain, negativity, and to prick you into a state of relaxation? Well, that's basically what EFT is all about; however, the needles are replaced simply with your fingertips. It also has the added benefits of rewiring thoughts and emotions due to your loving and uplifting affirmations and validation of feelings. It's a quiet time with yourself like no other, and if you're afraid of things that are sharp, it's a much better option than acupuncture.
- Ground yourself as you're moving about. Simply imagine your energy floating and sticking to the earth as you're walking, holding you down by your soles as you're standing in line, and so on. Staying connected spiritually, centering yourself, and sticking to the earth and realities of your life can become hard at times.
- Look after yourself by filling up on all your green (veggies and fruits included), and getting in all those skipped workouts. A healthy body is key in bringing forth vibrations into your field that recharges your heart and energy. You'll get healthy and positive in no time!

The Art of Smudging

Smudging is a ceremony that involves burning sage or other sacred plants, which strikes out negative thoughts, feelings, and energies that cloud the space within your field. It could be your emotional, energetic, mental, spiritual, or physical self or your surroundings; everything affects everything, and it's up to you to take care of it all and clear the smoke from your field.

To start, you'll need some sage or other form of sacred plant like cedar or sweet grass, an abalone shell, matches, a feather, and a drum or two. Clear out all the clutter, open up the windows and curtains, and allow the clean air and bright light to enter. Light your sage (or herbs) and fan the smoke with your feather around your body and the body of anyone else present. Once you've got everything ready and set to go, you can start getting down to the process. Now, you have some choices to consider and explore such as *Wapajea's Smudging Process* or that of Feng Shui. However, I will keep things general and simple for you to start off your journey:

1. Work your way around your home, moving in a clockwise direction, and ending where you started. Remember to move mindfully, with care, and slowly; give attention to all the nooks and crannies.
2. Direct smoke around and over any objects you feel need some attention, whether it be jewelry, clothing, mirrors, or other items that have negative memories and associations. Allow the smoke to flow and make its way around your home and space.
3. You can also chant a mantra or say a prayer that has meaning to you as a way to further fill the space with cleansing and positive vibrations and energies.

Reiki

Reiki is an energy healing technique that promotes relaxation and reduces stress through gentle touch. Reiki practitioners use their hands to deliver energy to your body and improve the flow and balance of your energy to support healing. You might experience the energy in the form of a warm, tingling, or pulsing sensation on the spots where the practitioner's hands are. However, most people generally feel relaxed, and might even fall asleep. Reiki sessions can be found all over, but ensure you search around for a trained and qualified practitioner.

Cleansing and healing your energy is of utmost importance because, without your energy in check, you might find it harder to not only develop and uphold your abilities, but to truly be who you're meant to be.

Cleansing Meditation

If only we could soak and scrub away all the energies and vibes we don't want or need. Well, this cleansing meditation is the closest we will get to doing just that!

Step One:

Create alone time in a quiet space, and set an alarm for about ten to fifteen minutes, longer if you want. You can sit with your legs crossed and hands on your knees, or lie down with your arms at your side. Close your eyes.

Step Two:

Take a few deep breaths, allowing yourself to relax and lose all other thoughts and struggles you have. Simply focus on the present and the way your body pulses with each breath you take.

Step Three:

When you're ready, focus on your toes, seeing them light up with a bright white light, and being cleansed of all tension and negativity. Feel the sensation of the energy leaving your skin and being filled with a cleaner, vibrating energy. With a loud *om* sound, repeat the following: "I cleanse my energy, release the negativity, and allow a new energy to take its place."

Slowly make your way through each body part until your entire body is beaming and vibrating with a bright white light. Know that your energy is clean and clear and that you have taken on new energy, a new start. Continue breathing and take your time to allow yourself to feel and appreciate the energy running through your entire body.

Step Four:

When you're ready, open your eyes and sit there for a few seconds, just breathing, and allow the warmth of your newfound energy to flow into your chakras.

What's Next?

Learning to heal and cleanse your energy is great, but what's even better is learning to protect it from getting damaged, clogged, and burnt from the start. It's important to protect yourself from the things and people that weaken you or lead you in the wrong direction. Find out more about this in the next chapter so that you can say goodbye to the worry of what might happen if you were to live authentically.

Chapter 10:
Protecting Yourself as an Empath

It was a hot and dry day in Bali, as most of the days in August were. Tourists crowded Kuta, although most were still asleep, recovering from the previous night's loud music, booze, and partying. Most nights in Kuta were like that, and tourists flocked to the experience. Jimmy, however, wasn't like that; he never really cared for the loud, crammed crowds, alcohol, and whatever else it held. He was there purely for the cultures, histories, experiences, and frankly, to get out of the house.

He still had a few stops to make and activities to take on, but for now, he was simply shopping around. He was looking for a souvenir to bring home to his mother after she had sworn she would be "madder than a wet hen" if he didn't. He knew his mother well enough to know she wasn't interested in traditional snacks, as the food at home was perfectly good. A silly trinket wouldn't do either, as it was too unthoughtful for her liking, although she would never say so. He had no idea what to bag up.

Jimmy sighed, window shopping the stores as he passed them, only giving some a quick glance before moving on. Why couldn't she just like keychains, ornaments, or t-shirts? he thought, groaning as the sun burned his skin. He figured he would buy himself a drink after hitting one more.

He looked up and, between the sharp rays of the sun, saw a poster plastered onto a shop's window that read: "Spiritual Gemstones on Sale!" Jimmy was intrigued by the mention of the so-called spiritual stones and had heard about them before, but he still couldn't tell you exactly what they were if you asked.

He figured he would give the shop a chance as his mother was always a great admirer of jewelry of all sorts. Besides, who can pass up a good sale? Jimmy strolled into the shop, taking in the store and the light-hearted, colorful atmosphere it had. Large rose quartz, clusters, and crystal balls filled various tables and some shelves of the store, while trays stood everywhere, stacked with extensive collections of crystals, rocks, and other minerals. Stocked in display cases were more crystals, fitted into necklaces and rings, or polished as they were. It was a beautiful place.

Jimmy browsed, searching for something he could see his mother wearing, when a man with a thick, frolicking coat walked up behind him to view a necklace with a tiny pink crystal enveloped in a silver coil.

"Ah, a Rose Quartz crystal, perfect for love and connection! A gift?" the man asked, slightly frightening Jimmy with his sudden appearance, which made the man laugh.

Jimmy nodded. "For my mom," he answered, knowing that he found the perfect gift. The man smiled, but also gave Jimmy a confusing look, before once again smiling and ushering Jimmy toward the counter.

"One more thing, my friend," he sang, pulling out a tray from one of the shelves and sifting through the pieces inside. "Here." He handed Jimmy a bracelet with three polished crystals adorning the middle. One was a bright yellow-y orange, like a freshly cut orange; the other was jet-black with a slight purple and gray hue; the last one was a faded dark purple.

Jimmy was instantly drawn to the piece, as if the crystals were vibrating energy toward him. It was beautiful.

"It will protect and shield you," the man explained, and before Jimmy could begin to object to the piece, the man interrupted. "I'll make you a deal: If you buy the special lady that necklace, you can have this one for free. Besides, you need it more than me." Jimmy looked at the man with a confused stare, not knowing that he was an empath left bare.

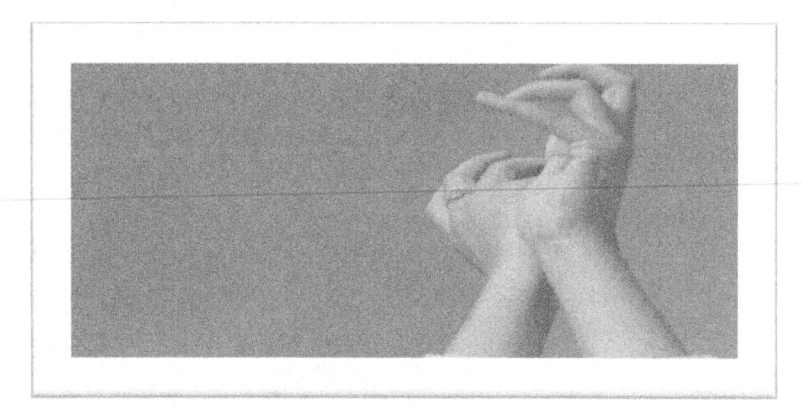

Things That Drain an Empath

Throughout this book, and in my previous book, *The Psychic Abilities of Being an Empath,* I have discussed things that overwhelm, drain, and negatively affect empaths. However, as my mother used to say, there's nothing wrong with a bit of a recap, so here you go:

- crowded rooms, loads of people, and bustling environments
- talking to people who bring them down or are stressed, angry, or down themselves
- loud noises, overwhelming scents, bright lights, and certain textures of clothing
- shocking news events, gruesome, distressing, or explicit movies and images
- shallow, meaningless, or negative conversations and conversation topics
- mental and physical exhaustion from overthinking, overworking, and taking on all the added baggage and loads of others
- no solid boundaries, or finding it hard to stick to them
- putting things off and procrastinating to avoid feeling overwhelmed

- feeling misunderstood by others due to your empathic nature and paired abilities
- you take on all the emotions of others, which also means the overwhelming feeling of negativity, confusion of your own emotions, and overload of information from others and yourself
- not knowing how to navigate being an empath, especially when it's not traditionally accepted in your family or social circle
- not knowing how to control your feelings and experiences, or how to develop and own your abilities

Signs That an Empath Is Burned Out

When life starts to seep in and build up until you can't take any more, you might find yourself overwhelmed and unsure about your own feelings, thoughts, and what you're going through and experiencing. You might feel that your day is going rather well; you were productive at work, had a nice day at home, and everything was looking good. Then, all of a sudden, you feel yourself slumping around the home, barely able to stand or cook, and you can't find a pinch of motivation or will to do anything but crawl back in bed. You're drained, whether you know it or not. So, here are some signs to look out for, so that you can get the rest you need for tomorrow to be a better day and stay that way:

- chronic fatigue
- self-medication
- mood fluctuations
- skin problems
- panic attacks
- aches, pains, and impaired immune system
- emotional and behavioral changes
- trouble staying focused
- missing out on previously enjoyable activities

- feelings of guilt or anger for taking on too many responsibilities
- feeling tired, anxious, or depressed

How to Protect Yourself

Learning how to walk the right line as an empath is an essential part of living your life and enjoying it as you should. You're a gifted individual, but with the empathic nature comes a whole set of challenges and struggles that others don't have on their shoulders. You're an empath, which in itself means that you not only see the world differently, but have to walk through it within a different light. Therefore, it's essential for you to keep your side of things clean, look after yourself, and protect yourself from what the world throws your way. Here's what you can do:

- detach yourself and isolate
- practice self-care and mindfulness
- be self-aware
- understand energies
- develop boundaries
- balance your nervous system
- develop emotional immunity
- learn to regulate intimacy
- ignore your inner critic
- practice self-compassion
- spend time outdoors
- find the time to recharge
- choose your people wisely
- keep a journal
- try visualization techniques
- create an empathic shield
- use protection tools like selenite, jewelry, and crystals
- practice deep breathing
- practice grounding

Protection Meditation

When it comes to your energy, emphatic nature, outlook and take on life, you need a bit more protection than most. Yet, even though you know this by now, it can be hard to know what it is you should do before you've got a shield to get you through. Luckily for you, however, there are meditations that work wonders.

Contrary to the meditations from previous chapters, this one takes very little prep, and you can do it at any time of the day, especially when you feel that your energy is being attacked, you're feeling overwhelmed, or you just need some added help to get you through the day.

Step One:

If it is not possible to go somewhere where you're alone, simply take a second to stand to the side, close your eyes, and take a few deep breaths to push yourself into a meditative state.

Step Two:

In your mind, or out loud, call on the spirit of the jaguar to protect you, and feel as her presence enters you. Continue breathing. Don't feel embarrassed or worried about what others are thinking, simply focus on yourself and the jaguar.

Step Three:

Visualize the creature as it strides around you, patrolling and encircling your energy while offering you its protection. Take in its beauty, its captivating, fierce eyes scouting for others, its sleek, graceful body purposely moving in a set path. Breathe as the jaguar continues its walk. Know that you're safe and protected. Thank the jaguar, and know that you can call upon that power whenever you need it again, whether it be today or another time. Continue breathing as you slowly begin to open your eyes and return to the real world.

What's Next?

Living as an empath can be a double-edged sword—it comes with both blessings and challenges. However, as much as it can be difficult, you must always remember that you have a gift. In a world where so many cannot express or process their emotions, being an empath can be your superpower that can save the world, including those around you and yourself.

Conclusion

As we come to the end of the book, note that you're only stepping into the start of your journey toward developing your abilities and accepting who you are. The road ahead might be a long and often challenging one; however, no one is more capable than you of taking it on.

We covered the grounds you need to finally understand what it takes to be an empath, who you are as an individual, and what it takes to develop your abilities and powers. You'll be able to fully embrace your gift and strive to use it for the greater good. You've been given the information, tools, and guidance to hopefully guide you to where you need to go and take the reins on the life you want to live.

Now is as good a time as any to embrace your superpower as an empath! Start maximizing your gifts and your unique input into this world. Be who you are.

Other empaths need your opinion!

Wouldn't it be a better world if more empaths were empowered? You can help achieve this by leaving a review and letting the book expand its reach. We need to stand together, after all, and help each other where we can. Remember that you're a warrior, so fight!

Please leave a review! (if you didn´t)

Click here if you bought the ebook:

https://geni.us/empathsebook

Or scan here if you bought the paperback:

Scroll to the bottom to find the "Leave a review option".

Remember: We are changing the world, one empath at a time! Thank you for your help!

Moving forward

If:

- *You need to work on your boundaries as an empath and learn how to do it without feeling guilty,*
- *You need to boost your self-esteem*
- *And find more ways to protect yourself.*

The best decision that you can make is to read this book. Invest this time in you! It is a practical guide, so you will have some fun and easy exercises to do, and believe me, you will thank yourself later!

Scan the QR code or click on the link to get your copy:

https://geni.us/empathspaperback

Let's connect:

If you still need to do it, join our Facebook group.

You will find like-minded people who want to grow together and want to thrive, not just survive.

https://www.facebook.com/groups/381006610842959

References pages

My book includes reference links that provide additional information, context, and credibility to the content. They demonstrate thorough research and allow you to delve deeper into the topics discussed, verify sources cited, and access related materials. Scan the QR code using your smartphone or tablet to access them.

Printed in Dunstable, United Kingdom